OPTILIFE PUBLISHING

Conquer Anxiety in 30 Days Using CBT

10 Powerful CBT Techniques to Beat Anxiety for Good & Reclaim Your Life

Contents

Bonus: Guided Meditation Audio Files

Enhance your journey with our exclusive Guided Meditation Audio Files. These meditations are designed to help you relax, focus, and achieve lasting tranquility

How to Access

1.Open your camera app on your smartphone.
2.Point the camera at the QR code below.
3.Tap the notification that appears to open the link.

Meditation 1 - Mindful Staircase

Meditation 2 - Journey Through Nature

Meditation 3 - Ancient Temple Exploration

Meditation 4 - Starry Night Sojourn

Introduction to Cognitive Behavioral Therapy (CBT)

Cognitive Behavioral Therapy (CBT) is a highly effective, evidence-based psychological treatment that focuses on the interplay between thoughts, emotions, and behaviors. It posits that negative thought patterns and maladaptive behaviors contribute to the persistence of psychological disorders, including anxiety. Through CBT, individuals learn to identify and challenge these negative thoughts and replace them with more rational, realistic ones, thereby influencing their emotional responses and behaviors towards more positive outcomes. Furthermore, CBT is distinct in its proactive, directive nature. Therapists collaborate with clients to set specific goals and work systematically to achieve them, making it a highly practical and structured approach to mental health improvement.

Understanding Anxiety: Symptoms, Causes, and Effects

Symptoms of Anxiety: Anxiety manifests through a combination of emotional, physical, and cognitive symptoms. Emotionally, it may involve feelings of dread or panic; physically, it can present as heart palpitations, sweating, and tremors;

cognitively, it may distort how a person perceives and reacts to their environment. The intensity of these symptoms can vary widely among individuals and may lead to behavioral changes like avoidance of certain places or situations, which can severely limit personal and professional life.

Causes of Anxiety: Anxiety can be caused by a variety of factors, including genetics, brain chemistry, personality, and life events. Stressful or traumatic events such as the death of a loved one, divorce, or job loss can also trigger anxiety disorders. Additionally, underlying health issues such as hormonal imbalances, side effects of medications, or chronic diseases can exacerbate or contribute to the development of anxiety symptoms.

Effects of Anxiety: Chronic anxiety can have a debilitating impact on an individual's daily life, affecting their ability to work, maintain relationships, and pursue leisure activities. Long-term, it can lead to physical health problems such as digestive issues, chronic respiratory disorders, and heart disease. On a psychological level, sustained anxiety can also lead to other mental health issues like depression or substance abuse, as individuals may seek relief from their symptoms through unhealthy behaviors.

How CBT Can Help Reduce Anxiety

CBT helps in reducing anxiety by breaking down overwhelming problems into smaller parts, making them easier to manage. It encourages a change in behavioral patterns and cognitive restructuring, where negative thoughts are challenged and replaced with more balanced views. This method not only alleviates symptoms of anxiety but also equips individuals with practical skills to handle future challenges more effectively. By focusing on the "here and now," CBT helps individuals reclaim their lives from anxiety. It also promotes a sense of empowerment, as CBT equips individuals with the tools to control their thoughts and responses, thereby enhancing their self-efficacy and overall mental health resilience.

Overview of the 30-Day Program

This book is structured around a comprehensive 30-day program designed to introduce readers to fundamental Cognitive Behavioral Therapy (CBT) techniques for managing anxiety. Each day will focus on a specific concept or skill, building cumulatively to provide a robust toolkit by the end of the month. The program is divided into four weeks, each with a distinct focus that progresses from basic skills to advanced applications and long-term strategies.

- **Week 1: Foundations of CBT** - You will learn basic techniques to identify and modify problematic thoughts and behaviors. This week lays the groundwork by focusing on essential CBT techniques such as identifying your anxiety triggers and understanding thought patterns.
- **Week 2: Developing Coping Strategies** - Focus will be on mastering skills to manage and reduce anxiety symptoms effectively. This includes advanced strategies like cognitive restructuring and problem-solving techniques that help

you tackle anxiety in a structured way.

- **Week 3: Advanced Applications** - You will integrate the skills learned into daily practices, enhancing your ability to cope with anxiety. The week will cover techniques such as behavioral activation and managing setbacks, enabling you to apply CBT skills more fluidly in everyday situations.
- **Week 4: Long-term Strategies and Maintenance** - The focus will shift to sustaining the gains made throughout the program and preparing for future challenges. This includes strategies for enhancing resilience and solidifying your support network.

Each day will include a mix of explanatory content, practical exercises, and reflective prompts to ensure a deep understanding and application of CBT principles. This structured approach will cover all **10 essential CBT techniques** over the weeks, allowing you to develop a comprehensive understanding of each and how they interconnect.

Flexible Scheduling: It's important to note that while this book provides a daily schedule, you do not have to strictly follow the plan each day. Depending on your progress, needs, or the complexity of the skills being practiced, you may choose to spend more time on one activity before moving on to the next. This flexibility allows you to fully engage with and master each technique at your own pace, ensuring that you derive the maximum benefit from each exercise.

This program is designed not only to reduce anxiety but also to promote overall mental resilience and well-being. By the end of the 30 days, readers are expected to not only have significantly reduced their anxiety but also to have a comprehensive understanding of how to maintain and continue building on these improvements independently. The ultimate goal is to empower you with the skills and knowledge to manage your mental health effectively over the long term.

I

Week 1: Laying the Foundation

"Every journey begins with a single step. Lay your foundation strong and the path will unfold." - Sienna Neel

Day 1: Identifying Your Anxiety Triggers (Technique 1)

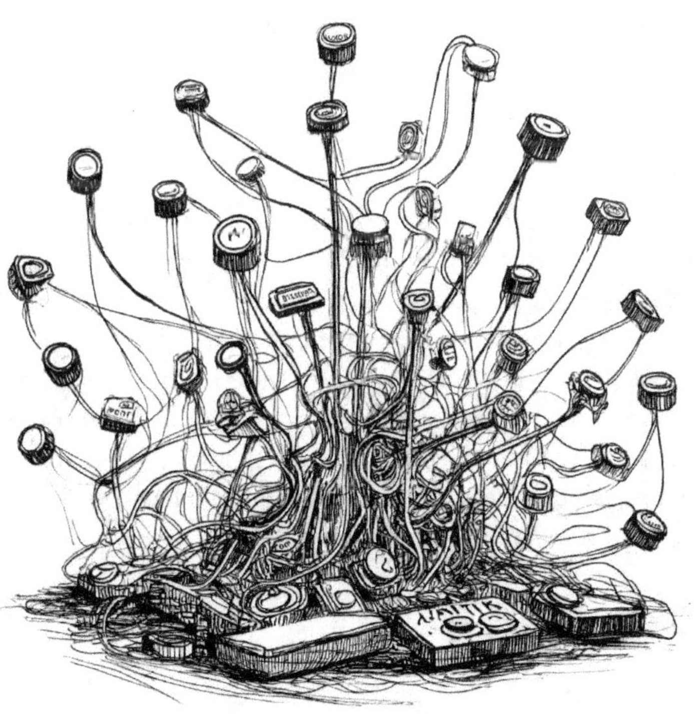

Objective

The first step in managing anxiety effectively through Cognitive Behavioral Therapy (CBT) is to identify what triggers your anxiety. Anxiety triggers can be specific situations, thoughts, or sensory experiences that precipitate an increase in anxiety symptoms. By identifying these triggers, you can begin to understand the patterns of your anxiety, which is crucial for later stages of CBT where you'll learn to challenge and neutralize these triggers. Understanding your triggers is also empowering—it shifts your perspective from feeling victimized by your anxiety to having active control over it.

Overview

Today, you will focus on recognizing the external events and internal thoughts that lead to feelings of anxiety. This may include specific people, places, responsibilities at work, family dynamics, or even broader concerns like health or financial issues. It's also important to be aware of the physical and emotional reactions you experience when faced with these triggers. By dissecting these experiences, you can start to distinguish between rational and irrational fears, which is a step toward regaining emotional balance.

Activity: Journaling Your Thoughts and Triggers

Purpose of the Activity: Journaling is a powerful tool in CBT for uncovering the hidden patterns in our thoughts and behaviors. By writing down your thoughts and feelings, you can gain clearer insight into what specifically triggers your anxiety and begin to see how your thoughts influence your emotional state. This reflective practice not only aids in self-awareness but also serves as a therapeutic tool, allowing for the cathartic release of pent-up emotions.

1.**Set a Regular Time and Place:** Choose a quiet place where you feel comfortable and can write without interruption. Make it a daily routine, perhaps in the morning to reflect on the previous day or in the evening as part of winding down. Establishing a consistent time and location for journaling helps create a habit, making it easier to integrate into your daily life. This routine becomes a dedicated moment for self-reflection and can significantly enhance the therapeutic benefits of journaling.

2.**Start with a Prompt:** If you're unsure where to begin, use prompts such as "Today I felt anxious when…" or "I noticed I started feeling anxious after…". These can help you start your journal entry. Prompts serve as a guide to focus your thoughts and can ease the challenge of facing a blank page. They encourage a deeper exploration of your emotions and behaviors, making your journaling session more productive.

3.**Describe the Trigger:** Detail the situation or thought that triggered your anxiety. Was it something someone said? A particular event or an upcoming responsibility? Describe the setting, the people involved, and what about the situation made you anxious. The more detailed your description, the better you'll understand the contexts and patterns that lead to your anxiety. This detailed accounting can help you in later sessions when you work on strategies to manage similar situations more effectively.

4.Record Your Physical and Emotional Responses: Note any physical sensations (e.g., heart racing, sweating) and emotions (e.g., fear, irritation) you experienced. This will help you connect bodily reactions with emotional states. Recognizing these signs early on can be crucial in implementing coping strategies before anxiety becomes overwhelming. It also aids in developing a more nuanced understanding of how your body and mind react to stress.

5.Reflect on Frequency and Intensity: Reflect on how often this trigger has caused anxiety in the past and rate the intensity of your anxiety on a scale of 1 to 10. This helps in assessing the impact of specific triggers on your well-being. Tracking these metrics over time can reveal improvements or worsening trends, helping you to gauge the effectiveness of the coping strategies you are implementing.

6.Review and Look for Patterns: After a week of journaling, review your entries to identify any recurring themes or triggers. This will be invaluable as you move forward with more targeted CBT techniques. Identifying patterns can illuminate underlying issues that may need more focused attention and can guide the customization of your treatment plan. Regular reviews allow you to adjust your approach based on real data from your own experiences, optimizing your strategies for better outcomes.

Conclusion of Day 1

Today's exercise is the first step towards gaining control over your anxiety. Identifying your triggers is an essential foundational skill in CBT, as it sets the stage for the more detailed work of challenging and changing your reactions to these triggers. Be patient with yourself during this process; self-discovery is key to effective anxiety management. As you continue to journal, you may find that your initial thoughts about what triggers your anxiety evolve, revealing deeper insights into your emotional triggers and how they manifest in your daily life.

NOTES

Day 2: Understanding Thought Patterns (Technique 2)

Objective

Day 2 of the program builds upon the initial understanding of anxiety triggers by delving into the thought patterns that typically accompany these triggers. The goal is to begin recognizing the automatic negative thoughts (ANTs) that often arise in response to anxiety-inducing situations. These ANTs can distort reality, amplify fears, and prolong anxiety, creating a vicious cycle that can be difficult to break without intervention. Understanding these thought patterns is crucial because they form the backbone of the cognitive aspect of CBT, where cognitive restructuring takes place.

Overview

Automatic negative thoughts are often irrational and unhelpful, and they can skew your perception of reality, leading to increased anxiety and stress. These thoughts are typically reflexive and not based on fact. Today's focus will be on identifying these thoughts, understanding their impact, and starting the process of learning to control them. By becoming aware of these patterns, you can challenge and change them, which is a central technique in CBT. Gaining insight into these automatic thoughts enables individuals to see how they contribute to emotional distress and to begin the process of replacing them with more adaptive thoughts.

Activity: Recognizing and Noting Automatic Negative Thoughts (ANTs)

Purpose of the Activity: This activity is designed to help you become more aware of the negative and often subconscious thought patterns that influence your emotions and behaviors. By recognizing these thoughts, you can begin to question their validity and gradually learn to replace them with more constructive and realistic thoughts. This is a crucial step in reducing the power that these automatic thoughts have over your mood and anxiety levels. The practice of identifying and altering these thoughts not only diminishes anxiety but also builds cognitive skills that are essential for long-term emotional resilience and mental health.

1.Identify the Thoughts: As you go about your day, pay close attention to any spontaneous thoughts that occur in response to situations that typically make you anxious. Write these thoughts down as soon as possible. Keeping a small notebook or a digital note app handy can make this easier and ensure you capture your thoughts in real-time. It's important to record not only the thoughts themselves but also the context in which they arise—note what was happening, who was involved, and how you felt at that moment. This will help you later analyze patterns and triggers in your thinking, providing crucial insights for cognitive restructuring.

2.Categorize the Thoughts: Understanding these distortions can help you recognize when your thoughts are moving away from realistic assessments and towards biased interpretations of your experiences. Here's an explanation for each type :

- **All-or-Nothing Thinking:** This type of thinking is also known as 'black-and-white thinking'. It involves seeing things in absolute, binary terms with no middle ground. For instance, if a situation isn't perfect, it's considered a total failure. This rigid way of thinking can lead to significant emotional distress because it leaves no room for error or learning from mistakes. People who frequently engage in all-or-nothing thinking may struggle with perfectionism and often feel dissatisfied with their achievements or relationships.
- **Catastrophizing:** This involves anticipating the worst possible outcome in a situation, even when it is highly unlikely. It's characterized by a tendency to magnify the potential consequences of an event, believing that if something can go wrong, it definitely will, and it will be disastrous. Such thoughts can provoke excessive anxiety and may prevent individuals from taking reasonable risks or trying new things due to an inflated sense of danger or doom.
- **Over-generalization:** This occurs when you take one

instance or example and generalize it to an overall pattern. For example, failing at a specific task might lead someone to conclude, "I always fail" or "I can never succeed," despite evidence to the contrary from other areas of their life. Over-generalization can create a negative self-fulfilling prophecy, limiting personal growth and fostering a negative mindset that overlooks positive outcomes and possibilities.

3.Challenge the Thoughts: For each thought, ask yourself a few questions to challenge its validity: Is there evidence that this thought is true? Is there evidence contrary to this thought? What would I tell a friend who had this thought? This process is crucial because it allows you to assess the accuracy and helpfulness of your thoughts critically. It's helpful to consider alternative explanations or outcomes that you may have overlooked. By practicing this regularly, you can begin to dismantle irrational or exaggerated thought patterns that contribute to anxiety and replace them with more balanced, rational thinking.

4.Record Emotional Responses: Note your emotional response to each thought. How do you feel when you believe this thought? Sad, anxious, angry? Recognizing the connection between your thoughts and feelings is key to understanding how your thought patterns influence your emotions. This step is not just about awareness but also about seeing the cause and effect in real time. By linking specific thoughts to emotional responses, you can start to identify which thoughts are triggers for negative emotions and begin to approach these thoughts more constructively.

5.Reflect on the Process: At the end of the day, review your notes. Reflect on how recognizing and challenging these thoughts affected your anxiety. Did the intensity of your feelings change? Did you notice any shift in how you reacted to situations after challenging your ANTs? This reflection helps consolidate what you've learned about your cognitive processes and their impact on your day-to-day life. It's also an opportunity to acknowledge your progress in managing anxiety, which can be very motivating. Reflection helps reinforce the benefits of the CBT techniques you are applying, making it more likely that you will continue to use them effectively.

Conclusion of Day 2: Understanding and modifying your thought patterns is a powerful skill in managing anxiety. Today's activity introduces you to the practice of cognitive restructuring, which will be developed further in the coming days. By continually practicing the recognition and challenge of negative thoughts, you can significantly reduce your anxiety and improve your emotional well-being. As you become more adept at this skill, you'll start to notice quicker and more effective changes in how you respond to previously anxiety-inducing situations. This exercise not only reduces the immediacy and intensity of anxiety responses but also encourages a habit of mindfulness regarding mental processes, enhancing overall mental health and self-awareness.

N O T E S

Day 3: The Basics of Mindfulness (Technique 3)

Objective

Mindfulness is a core aspect of Cognitive Behavioral Therapy (CBT) that helps you cultivate a state of active, open attention to the present. This day focuses on introducing you to mindfulness, teaching you to observe your thoughts and feelings from a distance, without judging them good or bad. The practice aims to break the cycle where habitual negative thoughts trigger a cascade of anxiety. By practicing mindfulness, you can learn to respond to stressful situations more calmly and rationally, thereby reducing the frequency and intensity of anxiety episodes.

Overview

Incorporating mindfulness into CBT can significantly enhance its effectiveness by reducing stress and improving emotional regulation. By learning to remain grounded in the present moment, individuals can observe their own thoughts and feelings as temporary and detached from their core self, which reduces their impact. This perspective is crucial in managing anxiety, as it helps to interrupt the automatic flow of negative thoughts and the emotional responses they provoke. Over time, mindfulness fosters a mental environment where one can approach life's challenges with more serenity and less fear.

Activity: Mindfulness Breathing Exercises

Purpose of the Activity: Mindfulness breathing exercises are a foundational practice in learning how to cultivate mindfulness. These exercises help you focus on your breath and teach you to return to this focus when your mind wanders. This practice not only calms the mind and body, reducing the physical symptoms of anxiety but also trains you to maintain awareness of the present, steering clear of ruminating on past events or worrying about the future. Additionally, regular mindfulness practice can lead to long-term changes in mood and levels of stress and anxiety, offering a powerful tool for emotional self-regulation and overall mental health.

How to Engage in the Activity:

1.**Find a Comfortable Position:** Sit in a quiet and comfortable place where you won't be disturbed. You can sit in a chair with your feet flat on the ground, on a cushion cross-legged, or even lie down if that's more comfortable.

2.**Focus on Your Breath:** Close your eyes and take a few deep breaths to begin. Then, let your breathing return to a natural rhythm. Focus your attention on the breath as it enters and leaves your nostrils, or focus on the rise and fall of your chest or belly. As you do this, try to notice the subtle sensations of the air moving through your nose, the slight coolness that accompanies each inhalation, and warmth upon exhalation. Feel the expansion and contraction of your diaphragm and lungs. This focused attention helps to anchor you in the present moment, diverting your mind from anxiety-producing thoughts and instilling a sense of peace and stability.

3.Acknowledge Wandering Thoughts: It's natural for your mind to wander. When you notice your thoughts have drifted, acknowledge where they went, then gently redirect your attention back to your breathing. This practice of recognizing thoughts and returning to your breath is the core of mindfulness training. Do not judge yourself or become frustrated with your wandering mind; this too is a part of the learning process. Each act of return enhances your ability to concentrate and strengthens your mindfulness. Over time, you may notice that interruptions by wandering thoughts become less frequent and your mind remains calm for longer periods. This practice is not only about maintaining focus but also about gently understanding the habit patterns of your own mind.

4.Duration: Start with a short session of about 5-10 minutes and gradually increase the duration as you become more comfortable with the practice.

5.Daily Practice: Consistency is key. Try to incorporate mindfulness breathing into your daily routine, even on days when you feel less anxious, to build a strong habit of mindfulness. As you grow more adept in mindfulness, you can explore other forms of mindful meditation and activities to enrich your practice.

Conclusion of Day 3

Today, you've begun to develop the skills to be present and mindful, an essential part of managing anxiety. Mindfulness breathing is a tool that you can access at any point in your day or whenever you feel overwhelmed by anxiety. It serves not only as a calming technique but also as a way to fundamentally alter your relationship with your thoughts. As you progress through the program, you will learn to apply mindfulness to a broader range of activities and thoughts, which will help deepen your ability to manage anxiety effectively. The more you practice mindfulness, the more you will find it beneficial not only in moments of anxiety but also in your everyday interactions and experiences, enhancing your overall quality of life.

NOTES

19

Day 4: Relaxation Techniques (Technique 4)

Objective

The objective of Day 4 is to introduce you to effective relaxation techniques, specifically focusing on progressive muscle relaxation (PMR). This technique helps reduce the physical symptoms of anxiety, such as muscle tension and shallow breathing, which are common responses to stress. By learning how to relax your body deliberately, you can control these physical anxiety responses, promote greater physical comfort, and decrease overall stress levels. Developing this skill not only aids in immediate stress relief but also contributes to long-term health benefits by mitigating the chronic effects of stress on the body and mind.

Overview

Relaxation techniques are essential tools in the treatment of anxiety, as they directly counteract the physiological arousal that characterizes anxiety. Progressive muscle relaxation involves sequentially tensing and then relaxing different muscle groups in the body. This contrast between tension and relaxation helps you become more aware of physical sensations and aids in deeper relaxation of the muscles. Over time, this practice not only improves your ability to relax quickly but also helps in the recognition and control of the physical manifestations of stress and anxiety. Incorporating regular practice of PMR can help normalize your overall stress response, making relaxation an automatic and natural counterbalance whenever stress levels begin to rise.

Activity: Progressive Muscle Relaxation

Purpose of the Activity: Progressive muscle relaxation (PMR) is a systematic technique that promotes overall body relaxation and reduces muscle tension. The activity aims to teach you how to relax your muscles through a two-step process: tensing each muscle group and then releasing the tension. This release can provide a profound sense of physical relaxation, which can, in turn, enhance mental relaxation. Practicing PMR can make you more aware of when you are experiencing muscle tension and help you develop a quicker reflex to engage relaxation techniques in response to stress. As this practice deepens, it also cultivates a greater mindfulness of bodily sensations and can enhance your ability to notice and address anxiety symptoms more rapidly.

How to Engage in the Activity:

1.Find a Quiet Place and Comfortable Position: Lie down on a flat surface or sit comfortably in a chair, ensuring your body is supported and you can relax fully without holding any muscle stiffly.

2.Tense and Relax Muscle Groups: Begin with your feet and work your way up to your face. Tense each muscle group (e.g., calves, thighs, glutes, abdomen, arms, hands, and face) for about 5 seconds, then relax it for 10 seconds. Pay attention to the sensation of releasing the tension and feel the muscles becoming loose and limp. When you tense each muscle, do so deliberately and strongly (without causing pain), which enhances your awareness of the contrast when you release the tension. As you relax, visualize the stress and tension melting away from the muscle group, and try to enhance the feeling of relaxation spreading throughout the area. This step not only helps in reducing physical tension but also trains your mind to recognize and differentiate between states of tension and relaxation, which is vital for stress management.

3.**Focus on Your Breathing:** Combine deep breathing with PMR for enhanced relaxation. Inhale deeply before tensing your muscles, and exhale when releasing the tension. This can help in maximizing the relaxation effect. Focusing on your breath serves as an anchor that keeps your mind engaged during the exercise, preventing it from wandering to stressful thoughts. The deep breathing technique also enhances oxygen flow to your muscles, which can help ease any discomfort caused by the tension and promotes a deeper sense of relaxation. By synchronizing your breathing with the muscle relaxation, you create a rhythm that can further deepen the relaxation response, making this practice more effective.

4.**Progress Through All Muscle Groups:** Move through each muscle group in sequence from your feet upwards to your head. Ensure to relax each group completely before moving to the next. Start by focusing on the smaller muscles in your feet and gradually work your way up to larger muscle groups. This systematic progression helps ensure that no part of the body is neglected and that the relaxation is comprehensive. Taking your time with each muscle group and not rushing the process is crucial for achieving a thorough relaxation. This methodical approach not only enhances your awareness of where you hold tension in your body but also ensures that by the end of the session, your entire body feels more relaxed and calm.

5.Reflect on the Experience: After completing the exercise, spend a few minutes in quiet, continuing to breathe deeply and enjoying the sense of relaxation throughout your body. Reflect on the areas that felt particularly tense and those that relaxed easily. Consider maintaining a log of your relaxation sessions to monitor your progress over time and identify any changes in your response to the technique.

Conclusion of Day 4

Today, you have learned how to effectively reduce physical tension through progressive muscle relaxation. This technique is invaluable for managing anxiety as it provides a practical method to quickly alleviate physical symptoms associated with stress. As you become more familiar with the sensation of relaxation, you'll find it easier to invoke this response during daily activities whenever you start feeling anxious. This skill is not only beneficial for reducing anxiety but also useful for improving sleep quality and reducing fatigue. Regular practice can transform this technique into a powerful, proactive part of your daily routine, offering a robust defense against the physical and psychological strains of stress.

N O T E S

25

Day 5: Creating a Worry Period (Technique 5)

Objective

The objective of Day 5 is to introduce a structured approach to managing worry by creating a designated "worry period." This technique helps prevent worry from consuming your day, allowing you to focus better on your tasks and engage more fully in your life. By confining worries to a specific time, you teach your brain to postpone the anxiety response, which can diminish the intensity and frequency of worrisome thoughts over time. It's a strategic approach that not only helps in controlling anxiety but also aids in enhancing mental clarity and emotional resilience by compartmentalizing stressors, making them more manageable.

Overview

Constant worrying can be draining and often interferes with daily functioning. The worry period technique involves setting aside a specific time and place each day where you allow yourself to focus on your worries. During this time, you can reflect on what's bothering you and even work on developing solutions. Outside of this period, you actively postpone worrying, which can help break the cycle of anxiety that disrupts mental peace and productivity. This technique leverages the principle that distancing yourself from continuous worry increases your capacity to deal with stress effectively when you revisit it with a fresher perspective.

Activity: Allocating a Specific Time to Worry

Purpose of the Activity: This activity is designed to help you gain control over your worry by confining it to a specific, limited part of your day rather than allowing it to spread uncontrollably. Allocating a specific time to worry reduces the 'background noise' of anxiety throughout the day, enhancing your ability to focus on other tasks and engage more positively in life. It also provides a structured time to assess the validity and importance of your worries, which often appear less overwhelming when revisited than when they first emerge. By systematically addressing these concerns, you can reduce their impact and develop more effective coping mechanisms.

How to Engage in the Activity:

1.Choose a Consistent Time and Place: Select a time and place where you can be alone and undisturbed, preferably later in the day so that worry does not overshadow your entire day. Limit this period to about 15-30 minutes.

2.Write Down Your Worries: During your worry period, write down what you are anxious about. This act of writing helps to clarify your thoughts and sometimes reveals solutions or mitigations you hadn't considered. The process of writing itself can be therapeutic, as it allows you to externalize what's on your mind and view it from a new perspective. Seeing your worries on paper can make them seem more manageable, rather than overwhelming. It also helps you detach from them, as you leave these worries confined to the pages of your journal or notepad, symbolically separating them from your mental space.

3.Review and Rationalize: Evaluate the worries you've written. Ask yourself if these worries are within your control, whether they are realistic, and what steps you can take to address them. This can help reduce the power they hold over you and lead to practical problem-solving. By questioning the validity of your concerns, you engage in a cognitive process called "cognitive restructuring," which is a core element of CBT. Determine what evidence supports or refutes your worries, and consider alternative interpretations. This rational review can demystify fears and reduce their intensity, providing a clearer path towards addressing them constructively.

4.Practice Postponing Worries: If you find yourself worrying outside the designated time, remind yourself to postpone the worry until your next worry period. This practice requires discipline but can significantly reduce the habitual anxiety that many people experience. Each time you successfully postpone a worry, you strengthen your mental control and flexibility, training your mind to deal with anxieties more on your terms rather than on their spontaneous emergence. Over time, this can lead to significant reductions in overall anxiety levels, as you learn to manage worries more effectively and confine them to specific, controlled periods. This skill of postponing can be particularly empowering, as it gives you a greater sense of control over your mental landscape.

5.Reflect on the Process: After your worry period, spend a few minutes reflecting on the session. Evaluate how it felt to contain your worries within a set time-frame. Over time, you may notice your designated worry time becomes less consuming and anxiety-inducing, as you become better at managing your thoughts. This reflection helps reinforce the benefits and effectiveness of the exercise, encouraging its regular use.

Conclusion of Day 5

Today, you've taken a proactive step in managing your anxiety by learning to compartmentalize and control your worrying. This technique is valuable because it acknowledges that while worries cannot be completely avoided, they can be managed more effectively. By gradually learning to restrict your worrying to a specific time, you're likely to find that many concerns are less urgent and significant than they might initially seem. This can lead to a more calm and measured approach to dealing with life's challenges. Adopting this method helps establish a healthier mental habit, where your energy is directed towards constructive problem-solving rather than being dissipated by constant worry.

NOTES

Day 6: Exposure to Triggers (Technique 6)

Objective

Day 6 introduces the concept of exposure therapy, a technique used in Cognitive Behavioral Therapy (CBT) to help individuals face and overcome their fears. The goal for today is to start with a gradual and controlled exposure to a mild trigger that causes anxiety. This approach helps in reducing the fear response over time by desensitizing you to the trigger, thereby lessening the anxiety associated with it. By systematically confronting your fears, rather than avoiding them, you can significantly weaken the associations that trigger your anxiety, enabling a more free and less constrained daily life.

Overview

Exposure therapy is based on the principle that avoiding feared objects, activities, or situations keeps the fear alive. By gradually and repeatedly exposing yourself to your fears, you can reduce your sensitivity to them, ultimately diminishing their impact on your life. This process can be challenging, but it is highly effective in treating various anxiety disorders, including phobias and panic attacks. Starting with mild triggers ensures a manageable and gentle introduction to this powerful therapeutic technique. As you become more comfortable with mild exposures, you'll gradually build the confidence to face more challenging fears.

Activity: Gradual, Controlled Exposure to a Mild Trigger

Purpose of the Activity: The purpose of this activity is to gently confront your fears in a controlled and safe environment, starting with something that elicits mild anxiety. This gradual exposure helps build confidence and resilience, as you learn that you can cope with anxiety and that the anticipated outcomes of your fears are often not as severe or catastrophic as imagined. This step-by-step approach not only lessens the emotional impact of the trigger over time but also reinforces the understanding that most anxieties are more manageable than they seem.

How to Engage in the Activity:

1.Select a Mild Trigger: Choose something that causes you mild anxiety, not severe fear. This could be speaking on the phone, driving on a highway, or attending a social event, depending on your personal anxiety triggers. It's important to start with a mild trigger to ensure that the experience is manageable and doesn't overwhelm you. This step is about building confidence in your ability to face your fears, not pushing yourself into distress. Consider triggers that are part of your daily routine but have consistently caused you some discomfort, as these will provide frequent opportunities for practice and mastery.

2.Plan the Exposure: Plan a short duration during which you will expose yourself to the trigger. For instance, if you're anxious about social interactions, plan to attend a social event for just 30 minutes or have a brief conversation with a stranger. Setting a clear time limit helps create a sense of control over the situation and assures you that the discomfort has a definite end point. This planning also involves choosing the right setting— one where you feel safe enough to face your anxiety but still challenged.

3.Prepare Mentally: Before the exposure, prepare yourself mentally by reviewing coping strategies, such as deep breathing or positive self-talk. Remind yourself of your objective and the controlled nature of this exposure. This mental preparation is crucial as it sets the tone for how you approach the challenge. Think through possible scenarios and how you will handle them. This can include planning your exit or who you will reach out to if you need support. Reinforcing your motivation for doing this exercise—such as the desire to overcome your anxiety and lead a fuller life—can also provide necessary encouragement.

4.Engage with the Trigger: Engage with the trigger at the planned time and duration. Stay in the situation until your anxiety starts to decrease, allowing you to experience the reduction in fear firsthand. It's essential to truly engage with the experience rather than just physically being present. Participate actively, use the coping strategies you prepared, and try to observe your reactions without judgment. This engagement is not just about enduring the situation but learning from it—identifying what aspects of the situation trigger your anxiety and noticing how your anxiety diminishes over time as you remain in the situation.

5.Reflect on the Experience: After the exposure, take some time to reflect on the experience. Note the level of anxiety you felt before, during, and after the exposure, and whether the actual experience was as challenging as you anticipated. This reflection can reinforce the learning and success of facing your fears. Consider jotting down your feelings and any thoughts that came up during the exposure in a journal, which can be a useful reference for future exposures.

Analyzing these notes can help you identify patterns or progress in your responses over time, giving you concrete evidence of how your reactions may be changing. It's also beneficial to assess what coping strategies were most effective and think about how you can apply them more efficiently in the future. This thoughtful review enhances your ability to manage similar situations in the future, gradually reducing your anxiety levels with each successful exposure

Additional Guidance for Each Step:

- When selecting a trigger, be sure to balance it carefully; it should be challenging enough to provoke a mild anxiety response but not so intense as to be unmanageable.
- During the planning phase, choose environments or times

where external stressors are minimized, ensuring the focus remains on the specific anxiety trigger.

- In mental preparation, reinforce your coping mechanisms by practicing them before the actual exposure. This could include visualization techniques where you imagine yourself successfully handling the situation.
- Finally, in the engagement phase, it's helpful to debrief yourself or with a therapist or a supportive person afterward. Discuss what you felt, what was particularly challenging, and what strategies helped the most.

By thoroughly engaging with each of these steps, you progressively desensitize yourself to the anxiety trigger, reducing its impact on your life and increasing your confidence and coping skills.

Conclusion of Day 6

Today, you've taken a significant step in tackling your anxiety by confronting a fear directly through exposure. This practice is essential for breaking the cycle of avoidance and fear reinforcement. With each exposure, you'll likely find that your anxiety becomes less intense and more manageable, which is a major achievement in regaining control over your life. This technique forms a cornerstone of effective anxiety management and will be built upon in more challenging ways as you progress in your therapy. Remember, the journey through exposure therapy is progressive; each step builds on the previous one, gradually leading to significant improvements in your ability to manage anxiety and fear.

NOTES

37

Day 7: Reflection and Review

The final day of the first week is dedicated to reflection and review. It's an opportunity to take stock of the progress you've made, to internalize the Cognitive Behavioral Therapy techniques you've learned, and to assess their effectiveness in managing your anxiety. This day is crucial for understanding how the different approaches have impacted you and for identifying areas that might need more focus or a different strategy.

Reflection is an integral part of any therapeutic process, especially in CBT, where understanding and modifying thought patterns and behaviors are key. It helps you see which methods have resonated with your personal experience and which ones may need adjustments to work better for you.

Today, you are encouraged to journal about each day's activities. Summarize what you did, how you felt, and any changes you noticed in your anxiety levels or overall mood. This activity not only helps solidify what you've learned but also provides a tangible record of your journey. As you write, try to pinpoint any techniques that were particularly helpful or any that didn't seem to make much of an impact.

Consider the emotional and physical reactions you experienced throughout the week. Were there certain days or activities that made you feel more anxious or more at ease? Identifying these can help you understand more about your anxiety triggers and what soothes them.

Look for patterns in how your anxiety has responded to the different techniques. Did your anxiety decrease as the week progressed, or were there significant fluctuations? Reflecting on the underlying reasons for these patterns can be insightful. It could be related to external stressors, your initial expectations, or how comfortable you felt with the process.

Finally, use today's reflections to set goals for the coming week. Decide which areas you want to focus more intensely on and consider how you can integrate the most effective strategies into your daily life. This proactive planning helps ensure that the therapy continues to be relevant and tailored to your needs.

Reflecting on and documenting your experiences from the first week not only celebrates your achievements but also sets the stage for the continuous improvement you aim to achieve through this program. As you move forward, these insights will guide you in refining your approach and focusing on strategies that offer the most benefit, enhancing both your confidence and your ability to manage anxiety.

II

Week 2: Developing New Skills

"Skills are the bridge between where you are and where you want to be." - Jim Rohn

Day 8: Cognitive Restructuring (Technique 7)

Objective

Day 8 marks the beginning of the second week, focusing on cognitive restructuring, a fundamental technique in Cognitive Behavioral Therapy. The goal is to identify, challenge, and change the negative thought patterns that contribute to anxiety. This technique helps you develop a more balanced and realistic thinking style, which can significantly reduce feelings of anxiety and distress. Mastering cognitive restructuring can transform how you process experiences and reactions, helping you adopt a more constructive and less reactive approach to challenges and stressors.

Overview

Cognitive restructuring involves recognizing and disputing irrational or maladaptive thoughts. It is based on the idea that negative thinking patterns, which often become automatic, directly influence our emotions and behaviors. By altering these thoughts, you can decrease the emotional impact they have and improve your mental health. This day aims to equip you with the tools to question and modify your negative thoughts, fostering a healthier, more positive mindset. The process is about building mental flexibility and enabling a shift from a pessimistic outlook to one that is more optimistic and grounded in reality.

Activity: Challenging and Changing Negative Thoughts

Purpose of the Activity: This activity is designed to practice the skill of cognitive restructuring. By actively challenging and changing negative thoughts, you can lessen their power over your emotions. The process not only helps in alleviating anxiety but also contributes to building lasting mental resilience. It encourages self-awareness and critical thinking about one's own cognitive processes, enhancing your ability to detach from and analyze thoughts rather than accepting them as truths.

How to Engage in the Activity:

1.**Identify Negative Thoughts:** As you go through your day, jot down negative thoughts as they arise. Focus on those that are recurrent and have a significant impact on your mood or behavior. This identification is the first step in breaking the cycle of automatic negative thinking. By becoming aware of these thoughts, you can begin to see patterns and triggers, which are essential for addressing them effectively. Keep a small notebook or use a digital note-taking app to ensure you can capture these thoughts as soon as they occur, making the process as immediate and practical as possible.

2.Analyze the Thoughts: For each thought, ask yourself several critical questions to challenge its validity: Is this thought based on facts or my feelings? Is there evidence that contradicts this thought? Are there alternative explanations for the situation that I haven't considered? This analysis helps to undermine the thought's credibility and reduces its emotional charge. By dissecting these thoughts and questioning their basis, you begin to weaken their hold over your emotional responses. This step is crucial in transforming how you interact with and respond to your internal narrative.

3.Reframe the Thought: Once you have challenged a thought, try to reframe it in a more balanced and realistic way. Instead of thinking, "I always mess things up," you might reframe it to, "Sometimes I make mistakes, but I can learn from them." This reframing helps to put things in perspective and fosters a more forgiving and productive mindset. It allows you to treat failures as learning opportunities rather than personal flaws, which can significantly alter your emotional well-being and increase resilience.

4.Reflect on the Changes: After reframing your thoughts, reflect on how this change in perspective affects your emotions and behaviors. Do you feel less anxious? How does changing your thought pattern affect how you approach similar situations in the future? Reflection solidifies the benefits of cognitive restructuring and encourages its continued use. It also helps you appreciate the progress you're making, reinforcing the positive impacts of these changes. Regular reflection can further enhance your ability to manage thoughts proactively and maintain mental agility.

Conclusion of Day 8:

Today's focus on cognitive restructuring is a vital step in taking control over how your thoughts influence your emotional well-being. By learning to recognize, challenge, and change negative thoughts, you develop a powerful tool against anxiety and improve your overall mental health. This process of cognitive adjustment is continuous and requires practice, but as you become more skilled in this technique, you will notice a significant improvement in how you feel and respond to challenges. This proactive approach to managing thoughts lays a strong foundation for more advanced CBT techniques you will explore in the coming days. As you progress, the skills developed today will become integral to your daily mental routines, enhancing not only your ability to handle anxiety but also improving your overall decision-making and problem-solving capabilities.

N O T E S

Day 9: The Role of Assertiveness in Reducing Anxiety

Objective

On Day 9, the focus is on understanding and practicing assertiveness as a means to reduce anxiety. Assertiveness training is vital in Cognitive Behavioral Therapy as it helps individuals express their thoughts, feelings, and needs directly, clearly, and respectfully. This skill is particularly beneficial for those whose anxiety is exacerbated by difficulties in interpersonal communication or a tendency to avoid confrontations. By becoming more assertive, you can significantly reduce stress and anxiety linked to communication in personal and professional settings. Enhancing your assertiveness skills not only helps in reducing anxiety but also contributes to building a more positive self-image and improving overall life satisfaction.

Overview

Assertiveness involves expressing yourself effectively and standing up for your point of view while also respecting the rights and beliefs of others. This balance is crucial in maintaining healthy relationships and self-esteem. For many people with anxiety, non-assertive behavior patterns such as passivity can increase feelings of anxiety and decrease self-confidence. By learning to be assertive, you assert your own worth, preferences, and needs in a manner that is socially acceptable and free from anxiety. Moreover, becoming assertive helps in setting clear boundaries, which is often a challenge for those who tend to prioritize others' needs over their own.

Activity: Practicing Assertive Communication

Purpose of the Activity: Today's activity is designed to enhance your ability to communicate assertively. This practice helps prevent the buildup of resentment and dissatisfaction that often results from non-assertive communication, which can contribute to anxiety and stress. Being assertive also enables you to handle conflicts more effectively and to foster better relationships, both of which can have a calming effect on your anxiety levels. Over time, regular practice of assertive communication will aid in normalizing these behaviors, making them more automatic and less stress-inducing.

How to Engage in the Activity:

1.Identify Opportunities for Assertiveness: Reflect on recent interactions where you were not assertive. Consider situations where you might have felt disregarded or overwhelmed. Use these reflections as the basis for today's practice. Analyze these scenarios to understand what prevented you from being assertive—was it fear of conflict, low self-esteem, or lack of preparation? Understanding these barriers can help you prepare more effectively. Think about how different the outcomes might have been had you expressed your thoughts and feelings more openly. This exercise is not just about identifying missed opportunities but also learning from them to better handle similar situations in the future.

2.Role-Playing: Engage in role-playing exercises with a friend, family member, or therapist. Practice how to express your needs and feelings clearly and respectfully. Focus on using "I" statements, maintaining eye contact, and keeping your voice calm and even. Role-playing helps simulate real-life interactions and provides a safe environment to experiment with different ways of expressing yourself. It can also help you receive direct feedback on your body language and tone, which are critical components of assertive communication. This practice builds confidence as you learn that you can express yourself without aggression or passivity.

3.Real-Life Application: Choose a real-life situation that you would typically find challenging. Apply your assertiveness skills by clearly stating your needs or opinion without being aggressive or passive. After the interaction, reflect on what went well and what you could improve. This step is crucial for transferring your learned skills into everyday situations. It might be daunting at first, but remember that each attempt at assertiveness, regardless of the outcome, is a learning experience. Notice how you feel during the interaction—more empowered, perhaps, or initially uncomfortable? Reflecting on these feelings will help you adjust your approach as needed.

4.Feedback and Reflection: After practicing assertive communication, seek feedback from the person you were interacting with or a third party observing the practice. Use this feedback to refine your approach. Reflect on how being assertive made you feel and whether it helped in reducing your anxiety. This feedback is invaluable as it provides an external perspective on your communication style. Ask for specific information about what aspects of your assertiveness were effective and which areas could use improvement. Consider this feedback seriously, and think about how you can incorporate the insights gained into your future interactions. This continuous loop of practicing, receiving feedback, and reflecting is key to mastering assertiveness.

Conclusion of Day 9:

Assertiveness is a powerful tool in managing and reducing anxiety, especially anxiety that stems from interpersonal interactions. By practicing and becoming more comfortable with assertive communication, you can enhance your self-esteem, reduce conflict, and improve your relationships. These improvements can lead to significant reductions in anxiety as you feel more empowered and less fearful in social interactions. Continual practice is key to becoming proficient in assertiveness, and each successful interaction builds confidence for future communications. As you move forward, keep reflecting on and adjusting your approach based on your experiences and the feedback you receive, solidifying assertiveness as a natural part of your interaction style.

N O T E S

53

Day 10: Problem-Solving Techniques (Technique 8)

Objective

Day 10 is dedicated to learning and applying problem-solving techniques to manage sources of anxiety effectively. This approach equips you with tools to identify, analyze, and resolve issues that cause stress and anxiety, promoting a sense of control and competency. By developing strong problem-solving skills, you can approach anxiety-inducing situations with a structured plan, reducing the overwhelming feelings that often accompany unexpected challenges.

Overview

Problem-solving is a critical skill in Cognitive Behavioral Therapy that involves a systematic process to address and mitigate problems that contribute to anxiety. It helps break down seemingly insurmountable issues into manageable parts, allowing for more practical and less emotionally charged solutions. This structured approach not only helps in dealing with the current issues more effectively but also enhances your ability to handle future challenges, reducing the overall impact of stress and anxiety on your life.

Activity: Applying Problem-Solving Steps to a Current Anxiety Source

Purpose of the Activity: Today's activity focuses on applying a step-by-step problem-solving method to a specific issue that is currently causing you anxiety. By systematically addressing the problem, you can reduce the anxiety associated with it and feel more empowered to take action. This activity encourages proactive behavior rather than reactive emotional responses, fostering a more rational and controlled approach to dealing with problems.

How to Engage in the Activity:

1.Identify the Problem: Clearly define what is causing you anxiety. Be as specific as possible—instead of a broad issue like work stress, identify a specific aspect, such as a challenging project deadline or a difficult coworker. Delving into the specifics helps isolate actionable elements of larger, more overwhelming problems. For instance, if deadlines are causing stress, consider what aspects of your time management or project planning could be contributing factors. Understanding the root causes of your anxiety in detail allows for more targeted and effective solutions.

2.Generate Possible Solutions: Brainstorm all possible solutions to the problem. At this stage, focus on quantity over quality, as the goal is to think creatively and consider all options, even those that might initially seem unrealistic. This open-minded approach can lead to innovative solutions that you might not consider under normal circumstances. Encourage thinking outside the box and resist the urge to judge ideas as they come—what seems impractical at first may lead to more viable solutions upon further exploration.

3.Evaluate the Solutions: Assess the feasibility, pros, and cons of each solution you have listed. Consider the potential outcomes and the impact they might have on reducing your anxiety. This step involves critical thinking and a realistic assessment of each option's practicality and potential effectiveness. Weigh factors such as required resources, time, and possible repercussions. This thorough evaluation ensures that the solution you eventually choose will be informed and well-considered, maximizing the likelihood of a successful outcome.

4.Choose a Solution: Select the most practical and effective solution based on your evaluation. It should be the one that best addresses the source of your anxiety while also being feasible and realistic to implement. This decision should take into account not only the direct benefits but also how the implementation could affect other areas of your life or work. Choosing the right solution involves balancing desired outcomes with potential trade-offs, ensuring that the benefits outweigh any costs or new challenges that might arise.

5.Implement the Solution: Put your chosen solution into

action. Prepare for potential obstacles and think about ways to overcome them. This step is about moving from planning to action, which requires preparation and adaptability. Consider creating a detailed action plan that includes timelines, responsibilities (if others are involved), and contingency plans for possible challenges that could arise during implementation. Effective execution is key to alleviating the anxiety associated with the problem, so focus on thorough preparation and proactive problem-solving throughout this phase.

6.Review the Outcome: After implementing the solution, reflect on its effectiveness. Did it help reduce your anxiety? What worked well, and what could be improved? This review is crucial for learning and for future applications of problem-solving techniques. Consider not only the immediate outcomes but also any long-term effects that may indicate the sustainability of the solution. Assess whether the approach can be adapted or refined for similar issues in the future, and think about any new skills or insights gained during the process.

Conclusion of Day 10

Mastering problem-solving techniques provides a powerful tool for dealing with anxiety. By learning to approach problems with a structured plan, you reduce the uncertainty and helplessness that often exacerbate anxiety symptoms. This day's activity not only helps in tackling current issues but also builds your confidence and skills for future problem-solving. Over time, these skills will become integral to your approach to challenges, making you more resilient and less prone to anxiety when faced with stressors. Keep practicing these techniques regularly to enhance their effectiveness and your proficiency

NOTES

Day 11: Avoidance and Safety Behaviors

Objective

Day 11 focuses on understanding and addressing avoidance and safety behaviors that are commonly used to manage anxiety but ultimately maintain or worsen it in the long term. The objective is to identify these behaviors and actively work on reducing their use in everyday situations. By confronting and reducing reliance on these behaviors, you can build true resilience and reduce anxiety more effectively. This step is essential for breaking the cycle of avoidance that limits personal growth and locks individuals into a pattern of fear and withdrawal from challenging yet enriching experiences.

Overview

Avoidance and safety behaviors are tactics used to escape or mitigate feared situations, such as avoiding public speaking or carrying anxiety medication "just in case" during outings, even when it's typically not needed. While these behaviors can provide temporary relief, they prevent individuals from fully engaging with life and learning that they can cope with anxiety without these crutches. Overcoming these behaviors is crucial for lasting anxiety management and recovery. The process involves a gradual stepping away from comfort zones, promoting learning and adaptation, which are vital for personal development and confidence building.

Activity: Identifying and Reducing Safety Behaviors

Purpose of the Activity: This activity is designed to help you identify and challenge the safety behaviors that you rely on to manage anxiety. The goal is to reduce these behaviors gradually, thereby increasing your exposure to anxiety-provoking situations in a controlled manner. This process helps you learn that the situations you fear are often less dangerous than perceived and that you are more capable of coping than you might believe. By systematically reducing these safety behaviors, you gain valuable opportunities to confront your fears directly, leading to a significant reduction in the power those fears hold over you.

How to Engage in the Activity:

1.Identify Safety Behaviors: Reflect on and list the behaviors you engage in to avoid anxiety or make yourself feel safer in anxiety-provoking situations. These might include avoiding eye contact, always sitting near exits, or over-preparing for meetings. Recognize that while these behaviors might provide temporary relief, they can also serve as barriers to truly facing and overcoming your fears. This realization is the first step in changing your response to anxiety-inducing situations, helping you to gradually regain control over your reactions and engage more fully in life.

2.Evaluate the Impact: Assess how these behaviors affect your life and your anxiety in the long term. Consider whether they prevent you from doing things you would like to do or if they reinforce your anxiety over time. Reflect on instances where these behaviors may have limited your opportunities— socially, professionally, or personally—and think about the broader implications for your happiness and well-being. This evaluation can motivate you to commit to change by illustrating the cost of safety behaviors not just to your mental health but to your life's quality and scope.

3.Choose One Behavior to Reduce: Select one safety behavior that you feel ready to challenge. Choose something manageable that does not overwhelm you but still pushes you to grow. It's crucial to start with a behavior that strikes a balance between being challenging enough to help you make significant progress and not so daunting that it sets you up for failure. Consider your current coping skills and support system when choosing which behavior to address first.

4.Develop a Plan: Create a plan for how you will reduce this behavior. Set clear, achievable goals. For example, if you tend to avoid making phone calls, you might set a goal to make at least one spontaneous call per week. Outline specific steps you will take to achieve this goal, and consider potential obstacles and how you might overcome them. This plan should also include strategies for managing anxiety that may arise as you confront these behaviors, such as breathing techniques or positive self-talk.

5.Implement the Plan: Start implementing your plan in a controlled manner. Monitor your anxiety levels and the outcomes of your actions. It's important to proceed at a pace that feels challenging yet achievable. Keep a journal or log to track your progress and any feelings or reactions that arise during the process. This documentation can be invaluable for understanding how your anxiety responds to different challenges and for adjusting your approach as needed. Celebrate small victories along the way, and use them as motivation to continue pushing your boundaries and reducing your reliance on safety behaviors.

Conclusion of Day 11

Today, you have taken important steps towards dismantling the safety behaviors that maintain your anxiety. This process is vital for experiencing and learning from situations that you typically avoid, which is essential for genuine and sustainable anxiety relief. Continue to challenge these behaviors gradually and consistently, as this will lead to significant improvements in how you manage anxiety and engage with the world around you. Each step forward in this journey enhances your ability to live more freely and assertively, opening up new possibilities for personal achievement and satisfaction. Remember, each small victory accumulates into substantial progress over time, leading to increased confidence and reduced anxiety. As you grow more comfortable facing previously feared situations, you'll find that what once seemed daunting becomes a source of strength and pride.

NOTES

Day 12: Using Imagery for Relaxation

Objective

On Day 12, the focus shifts to using imagery for relaxation, a powerful technique in Cognitive Behavioral Therapy that involves guided visualization to promote mental and physical relaxation. The objective is to harness the power of your imagination to create calming images and scenarios that can help reduce stress and anxiety. This technique is particularly useful for those who may find it challenging to relax through more traditional methods like deep breathing or meditation.

Overview

Imagery for relaxation utilizes the mind's ability to visualize places, situations, or experiences that are soothing and peaceful. By engaging the senses in detailed imagined experiences, you can elicit a relaxation response that has tangible benefits on both the mind and body. This practice can be especially beneficial before stressful events, at bedtime, or any time when anxiety levels are elevated. It helps in distancing oneself from immediate stressors and shifts focus to calming thoughts, thus reducing overall anxiety.

Activity: Guided Visualization

Purpose of the Activity: The purpose of this activity is to guide you through a visualization process that fosters deep relaxation. By creating vivid, peaceful images in your mind, you can engage your body's natural relaxation response and counter the physical and psychological effects of stress. This activity not only promotes relaxation but also improves your ability to concentrate and control your focus during times of stress.

How to Engage in the Activity:

1.Find a Quiet Space: Choose a comfortable and quiet space where you won't be disturbed. Make sure you are in a relaxing posture, either seated or lying down. This environment should feel safe and soothing, free from distractions such as noise, bright lights, or potential interruptions. The physical setting plays a crucial role in facilitating relaxation, as external calmness can encourage internal peace. If possible, use this same space consistently for your relaxation exercises to establish a routine and condition your mind to enter a state of relaxation more quickly when you are in this environment.

2.Close Your Eyes and Breathe Deeply: Start by taking a few deep breaths to initiate a state of physical relaxation. Pay attention to your breath and let go of any tension in your body. Focus on the rhythm of your breathing, inhaling slowly through your nose, holding for a moment, and exhaling through your mouth. With each exhale, imagine releasing stress and tension built up in your muscles. This not only helps to relax the body but also signals the mind to slow down and prepares it for the visualization process.

3.Visualize a Peaceful Scene: Imagine a place where you feel completely at ease. This could be a beach, a forest, a favorite childhood spot, or anywhere that you associate with peace and tranquility. Engage all your senses—notice the sounds, the scents, and the textures around you in your imagined place. Perhaps you can feel the warmth of the sunlight or the cool breeze against your skin. The more detailed and vivid the visualization, the more immersive the experience. By fully engaging your senses, you enhance the relaxation effect and make the scenario more real and effective in calming your mind.

4.Deepen the Experience: Enhance the visualization by adding elements that increase your sense of peace. Perhaps you hear birds singing, feel the sun on your skin, or smell the fresh scent of rain. Allow yourself to explore this space thoroughly, experiencing it as if you were truly there. Imagine interacting with this environment—walking along the beach, touching the cool bark of the trees, or tasting the fresh air. This active participation makes the visualization more dynamic and absorbing, helping to distract from any external anxiety triggers and deepen the sense of tranquility.

5.Slowly Return to Reality: After spending a few minutes in your visualized environment, gently bring your awareness back to the present. Notice the room you are in, move your fingers and toes, and open your eyes when you're ready. Transitioning smoothly and slowly out of your visualization helps maintain the calmness you've cultivated. Take a moment to reflect on the peaceful feelings and try to carry them with you as you resume your day. Each session of visualization should leave you feeling refreshed and mentally clearer, more prepared to handle the stresses of everyday life.

Conclusion of Day 12

Today's introduction to guided visualization has equipped you with a powerful tool for relaxation that you can access at any time. This technique not only helps manage stress and anxiety but also enhances your overall sense of well-being. As you practice this technique regularly, you'll likely find it easier to evoke feelings of calm during stressful situations. Continue to explore different scenarios and sensory details in your visualizations to keep the practice engaging and effective. This skill is not only useful for immediate relaxation but also for cultivating a longer-term resilience against stress.

NOTES

71

Day 13: Building a Support Network

Objective

Day 13 emphasizes the importance of building a support network, a crucial component in managing and overcoming anxiety. The goal is to foster connections with friends, family, or support groups who can provide emotional support, offer practical advice, and help you feel less isolated in your struggles. Building a robust support network can enhance your resilience, provide you with different perspectives on managing anxiety, and offer encouragement and motivation when facing challenges. Having a diverse range of support can also ensure that you have access to different types of help and information, which can be critical during moments when anxiety becomes particularly challenging.

Overview

A strong support network acts as a safety net during times of stress or crisis. It consists of individuals who understand your experiences or are empathetic to your situation. These connections can be instrumental in providing support that is both nurturing and practical. For those dealing with anxiety, knowing there are trusted people you can turn to can significantly alleviate feelings of fear and loneliness, making it easier to navigate difficult periods. Furthermore, building these relationships can also improve your overall mental health and well-being by increasing your sense of belonging and community, which are important factors in emotional resilience.

Activity: Reaching Out to Friends or Support Groups

Purpose of the Activity: The purpose of today's activity is to actively engage in expanding or strengthening your social support system. Whether reaching out to old friends, making new connections, or joining support groups, the aim is to increase your network of support, which can play a vital role in your journey toward managing anxiety. Establishing these connections can also provide new opportunities for sharing experiences and strategies that might be effective in managing similar challenges, thereby broadening your own toolkit for anxiety management.

How to Engage in the Activity:

1.**Identify Potential Supporters:** Make a list of people you already know who are understanding, compassionate, and supportive. Think about how you might deepen those relationships. Additionally, identify groups or communities that align with your interests or experiences related to anxiety management.

To find these groups, you can start by looking online. Websites like Meetup.com offer a variety of local and virtual groups focused on mental health and wellness. Social media platforms, such as Facebook and LinkedIn, also host numerous groups where members share experiences and support each other in anxiety management.

Another excellent resource is local community centers or health clinics, which often offer support groups or workshops on managing anxiety. You might also consider contacting mental health organizations like the Anxiety and Depression Association of America (ADAA), which can direct you to both resources and support groups. Universities or hospitals are also key places that frequently offer therapy groups or anxiety workshops open to the public

2.Initiate Contact: Reach out to these individuals or groups. This could be through a phone call, a text message, an email, or attending a meeting or social event. Express your interest in connecting or reconnecting, and be open about your intention to build a supportive network. Be genuine in your communications and express appreciation for any positive past interactions you may have had. If you feel anxious about reaching out, remember that many people feel flattered by genuine interest and connection attempts. Start with something simple and non-demanding; a brief message or a query about joining an existing group activity can open doors without too much pressure on either side.

3.Participate Actively: Engage actively with the people or groups you reach out to. Share your experiences, listen to others, and participate in discussions or activities. Being actively involved helps to solidify your connections and ensures that the relationships are mutually beneficial. It's also a chance to practice social skills in a supportive environment, which can be particularly beneficial for those with social anxiety. Offer to contribute in ways that align with your strengths— whether it's helping organize an event, contributing knowledge, or supporting others in the group. Active participation not only enriches your experience but also makes you a valuable member of any social circle.

4.Establish Regular Communication: Try to establish regular communication with your support network. Set up recurring meet-ups, phone calls, or online chats to maintain these connections. Consistency helps to build trust and familiarity, which are essential for a supportive relationship. Regular interaction also keeps the lines of communication open for times when you might need support unexpectedly. If scheduling regular meet-ups is challenging, consider using digital tools like group chats or social media groups to stay in touch. Regular updates, even if brief, can help maintain the bond and ensure that you feel connected even when life gets busy.

Conclusion of Day 13

Today, you have taken significant steps toward building or strengthening your support network. This network will be invaluable as you continue to manage your anxiety, providing emotional support and practical advice. Remember, building relationships takes time and effort, but the rewards are substantial. A strong support network not only provides comfort and encouragement but also enriches your life, making your journey through anxiety management more bearable and less lonely. As you nurture these relationships, they become a source of strength and comfort that you can rely on, enhancing both your ability to cope with anxiety and your overall life satisfaction.

NOTES

Day 14: Reflection and Review

The second week concludes with a day dedicated to reflection and review. This time allows you to look back on the development of new skills such as cognitive restructuring, assertiveness, problem-solving techniques, and the use of imagery for relaxation. By reflecting on these practices, you can assess their impact on your anxiety levels, enhance your understanding of which techniques work best for you, and plan how to integrate these skills more effectively into your daily life.

Reflecting on each skill learned over the week helps to consolidate the knowledge and practice gained. This process is essential for making the transition from learning and practicing skills in a structured setting to applying them in real-world scenarios. It's a time to appreciate the progress made and to recognize areas that might need more attention or a different approach.

Reflect on the Week's Progress and Journal Insights:

1.Summarize Each Day's Focus: Start by revisiting each day's main focus and activities. Write about your experiences with cognitive restructuring on Day 8, your efforts to be more assertive on Day 9, your application of problem-solving techniques on Day 10, and your practice of guided visualization on Day 12. Reflect on how engaging with these activities felt and how they impacted your daily routines. Consider the immediate responses you had to these exercises and any new understandings or changes in perspective that emerged from each session.

2.Evaluate Your Experiences: Consider how these activities affected your anxiety and overall mental state. Which techniques were most effective? Did any of the skills learned this week help in reducing your anxiety more than others? Take time to assess not only the short-term effects, such as momentary relief from anxiety, but also any long-term changes in your emotional resilience or coping strategies. Evaluate whether some techniques were more practical or easier to integrate into your daily life than others, and reflect on how each technique helped to address different aspects of your anxiety.

3.Identify Patterns and Insights: Look for patterns in how you responded to different techniques. Did certain skills resonate more with you or prove more challenging to implement? Understanding these patterns can guide your continued practice and highlight which skills need further development. For instance, you might notice that techniques involving active problem-solving gave you a sense of control, whereas techniques requiring passive observation were more difficult. Recognizing these preferences and challenges can help tailor your ongoing therapeutic practices to be more effective and engaging.

4.Plan for Future Application: Based on your week's experiences, identify areas where continued practice is needed. Plan how you might incorporate the most useful techniques into your routine more seamlessly. For example, you might decide to use cognitive restructuring regularly when faced with stress at work or to engage in guided visualization before sleep to improve relaxation. Think about practical ways to make these techniques part of your everyday life, such as setting reminders to practice or integrating brief sessions into your morning or evening routines.

5.Set Goals for the Upcoming Week: Outline specific goals for the next week. These could include practicing assertiveness in a particular challenging situation, scheduling daily times for problem-solving, or deepening your visualization practice by exploring new scenarios. Make these goals specific, measurable, and tied to real-life activities to increase your chances of success. For instance, you might set a goal to assertively express your needs in at least two work meetings, or to spend 15 minutes each evening dedicated to solving a recurring problem in your personal life. Setting concrete goals will help maintain your momentum and ensure continuous improvement in managing your anxiety.

Conclusion of Day 14

Reflecting on your experiences and documenting them enhances your learning and prepares you for continued progress in your journey through CBT. This review not only helps you understand what has been effective but also empowers you to take control of your therapy going forward. As you prepare for the upcoming week, use today's insights to refine your approach, focusing on areas where you've seen the most improvement and those that still present challenges. The skills developed during this week form a crucial part of your toolkit for managing anxiety and building a healthier, more balanced life.

III

Week 3: Strengthening CBT Techniques

"Strength doesn't come from what you can do. It comes from overcoming the things you once thought you couldn't." - Rikki Rogers

Day 15: Introducing Behavioral Activation (Technique 9)

Objective

Day 15 introduces Behavioral Activation, a crucial component of Cognitive Behavioral Therapy that focuses on engaging actively in enjoyable activities to combat the inertia often caused by depression and anxiety. The goal is to schedule and participate in activities that you find pleasurable or fulfilling, which can significantly enhance your mood and energy levels. Behavioral Activation helps break the cycle of avoidance and withdrawal that can exacerbate symptoms of depression and anxiety by promoting engagement and satisfaction in everyday life. This shift from passivity to activity encourages not only psychological but also physical benefits, as increased activity levels can improve overall health and vitality.

Overview

Behavioral Activation is based on the theory that, by avoiding activities, individuals may unintentionally worsen their depression and anxiety. This avoidance usually results in decreased opportunities for positive reinforcement and an increased sense of isolation and dissatisfaction. By identifying and engaging in valued or enjoyable activities, you can shift this dynamic, increasing positive experiences and feelings, which contribute to improved mood and reduced anxiety. This technique is particularly effective because it encourages a proactive approach to managing mood states through action, which also builds a greater sense of control and self-efficacy.

Activity: Planning Enjoyable Activities

Purpose of the Activity: The purpose of today's activity is to identify activities that bring joy, relaxation, or a sense of achievement and incorporate them into your daily or weekly routine. By planning and committing to these activities, you can increase your engagement with life, counteract feelings of sadness or anxiety, and build a more positive outlook. Engaging regularly in activities that you enjoy can also create a buffer against the stress and strain of daily life, providing regular doses of pleasure that can keep negativity at bay.

How to Engage in the Activity:

1.Identify Enjoyable Activities: Make a list of activities that you enjoy or have enjoyed in the past. These can range from hobbies, social events, sports, artistic pursuits, or simple pleasures like reading a book or walking in nature. Try to include a variety of activities that cater to different aspects of your well-being—physical, emotional, and social. When making your list, think about activities that make you lose track of time or those that leave you feeling energized or more relaxed afterward. Including both individual and group activities can also help balance your need for solitude with social interaction, enriching your overall life experience.

2.Set Specific Goals: Choose a few activities from your list that you can realistically integrate into your upcoming week. Set specific, achievable goals for each. For example, if you enjoy painting, schedule a two-hour session for your next project. Setting these goals not only commits you to action but also gives you something to look forward to, which can be incredibly motivating. Be sure to consider your current schedule and commitments to avoid overloading yourself. It's better to start with small, manageable goals that can be easily achieved and gradually build up as you find more time and confidence.

3.Prepare for Success: Ensure you have everything needed to successfully engage in the chosen activities. This might involve gathering materials, coordinating with others, or setting reminders. Preparation is key to making sure that planned activities actually happen and are enjoyable, rather than becoming sources of stress themselves. Check in advance to ensure you have the necessary supplies or confirm arrangements with others if the activity involves group participation. This foresight can prevent last-minute scrambles and help you approach your leisure time with a calm, prepared mindset.

4.Engage in the Activities: Follow through with your plans. As you engage in each activity, take a moment to be fully present, savoring the experience and noting how it affects your mood and energy levels. This mindfulness element can enhance the enjoyment and benefits of the activity. Avoid multitasking during these moments; focus solely on the activity at hand, whether it's painting, reading, or taking a walk. Paying attention to the details of the experience can greatly increase its restorative effects and make your leisure time more fulfilling.

5.Reflect on the Experience: After completing each activity, reflect on how it made you feel. Did it improve your mood? Did it reduce your anxiety? Use this information to adjust your future plans, possibly incorporating more or similar activities into your routine. Reflecting on your emotional responses can help you fine-tune your activity choices to maximize their therapeutic benefits. Consider keeping a journal of these reflections, which can help you track your feelings and identify which activities offer the most benefits, thereby guiding your future choices in how you spend your free time.

Conclusion of Day 15

Today, you have taken significant steps by introducing Behavioral Activation into your routine. This approach is essential for combating the passive tendencies that often accompany anxiety and depression. As you continue to engage in enjoyable activities, you'll likely notice an uplift in your mood and a decrease in anxiety levels, reinforcing the benefits of an active, engaged lifestyle. These activities not only enhance your day-to-day life but also bolster your long-term resilience against mental health challenges. Keep experimenting with different activities to keep your routine enjoyable and effective at boosting your mood, and remember, the goal is to create a sustainable habit that supports your mental health and overall well-being.

* * *

Unlock the Power of Change

Make a Difference with Your Review

"One of the most beautiful compensations in life is that no one can sincerely try to help another without helping themselves." - **Ralph Waldo Emerson**

People who manage their anxiety effectively live longer, happier lives and achieve more of their goals. If there's a chance to help someone else find that peace during our time together, then I'm committed to trying.

To make that happen, I have a question for you…

Would you help someone you've never met, even if you never got credit for it?

Who is this person, you ask? They are like you. Or, at least, like you used to be. Less experienced in managing anxiety, eager to make a change, and needing help, but not sure where to look.

Our mission is to make "effective anxiety management" accessible to everyone. Everything we do stems from that mission. And the only way for us to accomplish that mission is by reaching… well…everyone.

This is where you come in. Most people do, in fact, judge a book by its cover (and its reviews). So here's my ask on behalf of someone struggling with anxiety who you've never met:

Please help that person by leaving this book a review.

Your gift costs no money and less than 60 seconds to make real, but it can change a fellow reader's life forever. Your review could help…

…one more person find relief from their anxiety.
   …one more reader support their mental health journey.
   …one more individual get the help they need to improve their life.
   …one more family experience the benefits of a calm and balanced member.
   …one more dream of living anxiety-free come true.

To get that 'feel good' feeling and help this person for real, all you have to do is…and it takes less than 60 seconds…

leave a review.

Simply scan the QR code or click the link below to leave your review:

» Click here to leave your review on Amazon or scan the QR Code below.

If you feel good about helping someone manage their anxiety, you are my kind of person. Welcome to the club. You're one of us.

Thank you from the bottom of my heart. Now, back to our regularly scheduled programming.

-Your biggest fan, ProPlan Publication

PS - Fun fact: If you provide something of value to another person, it makes you more valuable to them. If you'd like goodwill straight from another reader - and you believe this book will help them - send this book their way.

NOTES

Day 16: Setting Realistic Goals

Objective

Day 16 is focused on setting realistic goals, an essential skill in managing expectations and achieving measurable progress in both personal and professional contexts. The objective today is to learn how to formulate goals that are not only achievable but also motivating and tailored to enhance your mental health. Realistic goal-setting can help mitigate feelings of overwhelm and frustration that often accompany overly ambitious or vaguely defined objectives, thereby reducing anxiety and increasing a sense of accomplishment. Understanding how to set realistic goals also teaches you to evaluate your current resources, capabilities, and time constraints, leading to more thoughtful and sustainable planning.

Overview

Setting realistic goals involves defining clear, attainable objectives that are directly aligned with one's capabilities and current circumstances. It helps in breaking down larger, more daunting tasks into smaller, manageable steps, which can be particularly beneficial for individuals dealing with anxiety or depression. This approach encourages gradual progress and celebrates small victories, which can significantly boost self-esteem and momentum in therapy. By consistently achieving these smaller goals, you build confidence and competence, which are vital for long-term success and personal growth.

Activity: SMART Goal Setting

Purpose of the Activity: Today's activity involves using the SMART criteria to set goals. SMART stands for Specific, Measurable, Achievable, Relevant, and Time-bound. This method ensures that goals are well-defined and within reach, which can increase your chances of success and reduce anxiety related to uncertainty or failure. By setting SMART goals, you can foster a sense of control over your life and direct your efforts more efficiently. This structured approach also helps in identifying which goals are truly important to you, ensuring that your efforts are spent on valuable pursuits that reflect your personal values and long-term aspirations.

How to Engage in the Activity:

1.Identify a Goal Area: Start by identifying an area of your life where you want to improve or achieve something specific. This could be related to personal health, work, relationships, or hobbies. Think about aspects of your life that have been lingering in your thoughts recently or areas you feel passionate about improving. Reflect on what changes in these areas would mean for your overall happiness and well-being.

2.Make it Specific: Define your goal as clearly as possible. Instead of "I want to be healthier," specify what being healthier looks like for you, such as "I want to jog three times a week." The more specific you are, the easier it will be to plan actionable steps and track your progress. Specific goals help eliminate ambiguity and make your intentions concrete.

3.Ensure it is Measurable: Include precise amounts, dates, and other measurable details. For the jogging example, you could define success as "jogging 30 minutes each session." By quantifying your goals, you create clear criteria for success, which will help you evaluate your progress and know exactly when you've achieved your objective.

4.Keep it Achievable: Make sure your goal is realistic given your current abilities and constraints. If you've never jogged regularly before, starting with three times a week might be too ambitious. Perhaps begin with once a week. Assess your current situation realistically—consider factors like your schedule, physical condition, and previous experiences to set a goal that is challenging yet attainable.

5.Make it Relevant: Ensure the goal is important to you and that achieving it will make a meaningful difference in your life. This increases your motivation and commitment to achieving the goal. Choose goals that align with your values and long-term objectives; this alignment ensures that the effort you put in feels worthwhile and keeps you motivated during challenging times.

6.Set a Time Frame: Decide on a timeline for achieving your goal. Having a deadline increases your sense of urgency and can help keep you focused. For jogging, you might aim to achieve this routine consistently for a month. A defined time frame prevents procrastination, helping you to structure your activities and prioritize your tasks effectively. It also provides a clear endpoint to work towards, which can be highly motivating.

Conclusion of Day 16

By setting SMART goals today, you have taken a structured approach to achieve tangible improvements in your life. This activity not only helps streamline your efforts towards more focused outcomes but also enhances your ability to manage and reduce anxiety by providing clear, realistic expectations. Setting SMART goals helps you organize your activities in a way that is optimal for mental health, providing a clear pathway to success and allowing for adjustments as needed. As you continue to practice these techniques, they will become an integral part of your daily planning process, helping you to achieve both immediate tasks and long-term objectives more effectively.

NOTES

Day 17: Gratitude and Positive Thinking

Objective

Day 17 is centered on cultivating gratitude and positive thinking, essential components in the psychological toolkit for combating negative mental patterns that contribute to anxiety and depression. The objective today is to develop an attitude of gratitude, which research has shown to significantly improve psychological well-being. By focusing on gratitude, you shift your attention from what is lacking or problematic to what is present and positive in your life, fostering a more optimistic outlook and enhancing overall happiness. This shift can also lead to increased energy, inspiration, and motivation, as focusing on positive elements naturally enhances one's overall perspective on life.

Overview

Gratitude and positive thinking are powerful tools for altering your psychological landscape. Emphasizing the positive aspects of life can transform your perception, mood, and interactions with others. By actively acknowledging the good in your life, you can diminish the space occupied by negative thoughts and feelings. This practice not only improves your mood and reduces stress, but it also strengthens your resilience by enhancing your capacity to cope with daily challenges in a more positive and proactive way. Moreover, fostering a gratitude mindset can improve relationships, as expressing appreciation to others tends to enhance mutual respect and communication.

Activity: Keeping a Gratitude Journal

Purpose of the Activity: The purpose of this activity is to develop a consistent practice of recognizing and recording the positive aspects of your day-to-day life. Keeping a gratitude journal involves regularly writing down things for which you are grateful, no matter how big or small. This practice trains your mind to notice and appreciate the positives more readily, which can shift your overall mindset from one of deficiency to one of abundance. Over time, this habit can profoundly alter your mental health, leading to greater contentment and a more joyful approach to daily life.

How to Engage in the Activity:

1.Choose a Journal: Select a notebook or digital app where you will keep your gratitude entries. Choose something that feels personal and pleasant to use. Opt for a journal that you feel drawn to, perhaps one with a design that uplifts your spirit or a digital format that is convenient and engaging. The aesthetics of your journal, whether it's the tactile feel of the paper or the user-friendly interface of an app, can enhance your commitment to maintaining this practice. A journal that resonates with you on a personal level can make the act of writing more enjoyable and something you look forward to each day.

2.Set a Routine: Decide on a specific time each day to write in your journal. Many people find it helpful to do this at the end of the day so they can reflect on the day's events, but the morning can also be a perfect time to set a positive tone for the day ahead. Consistency is key in building this habit, so choose a time that fits naturally into your daily schedule. Aligning this practice with other daily routines, such as having morning coffee or before bedtime rituals, can help integrate gratitude journaling seamlessly into your life, making it less of a chore and more of a cherished habit.

3.Record Grateful Thoughts: Each time you write, list at least three things for which you are grateful. These can range from significant events like a job promotion to everyday pleasures like a good cup of coffee or a call from a friend. Try to vary your entries and include different aspects of your life to maintain a broad perspective on the many sources of joy around you. By acknowledging a wide array of positives, from the mundane to the extraordinary, you cultivate a deeper appreciation for life's diversity and the multitude of blessings that can often go unnoticed.

4.Elaborate When Possible: Whenever you can, add a sentence or two explaining why you're grateful for each item. This deepens the feeling of gratitude and reinforces the positive emotions associated with it. Elaborating on your gratitude can help clarify your values and priorities, which can guide future actions and decisions. The act of expanding on your gratitude helps to anchor these feelings more deeply within your psyche, enhancing the psychological benefits of this practice and making gratitude a more integral part of your thought processes.

5.Reflect on the Changes: Periodically, look back on your entries to see how your thoughts have shifted over time. This reflection can be incredibly uplifting and motivating, as you realize just how many positive things occur in your life regularly. It also allows you to observe patterns in what brings you joy and satisfaction, potentially guiding you toward further beneficial activities and relationships. Seeing your growth and change through the lens of gratitude can also provide a resilient buffer against times of stress or sadness, reminding you of the good that persists even in difficult times.

Conclusion of Day 17

Engaging in gratitude journaling today has set the foundation for a habit that can significantly enhance your psychological health. This simple but profound practice encourages a shift towards more positive thinking and can dramatically improve your emotional well-being. As you continue with this activity, you might find that your overall outlook becomes more hopeful and that challenges seem more manageable. Keep building on this practice, and allow the growing sense of gratitude to permeate all aspects of your life, enhancing both your mental health and your interactions with others. Each entry serves as a reminder of the good in your world, reinforcing a positive mindset that can endure beyond moments of difficulty.

NOTES

Day 18: Managing Setbacks (Technique 10)

Objective

Day 18 focuses on managing setbacks, an inevitable part of any journey toward personal growth and recovery. The objective today is to acknowledge that setbacks are normal and to develop strategies for coping effectively when they occur. By planning how to handle setbacks, you can minimize their impact and prevent them from derailing your progress. This proactive approach helps maintain momentum in your therapy and ensures that you remain resilient in the face of challenges. Understanding that setbacks are not permanent or reflective of your capabilities but rather are opportunities for learning and adaptation enhances your ability to navigate them without significant distress.

Overview

Setbacks can be discouraging and may lead to feelings of failure or frustration. However, viewing these experiences as natural parts of the learning process can change your perception of setbacks from being failures to being opportunities for growth. This shift in perspective is crucial for building long-term resilience and for fostering a more forgiving and patient attitude towards yourself. Learning to manage setbacks effectively also prevents the cycle of negative thinking that can intensify feelings of anxiety and depression. Embracing setbacks as part of the journey allows you to deal with them more calmly and productively, facilitating quicker recovery and adaptation.

Activity: Developing a Coping Plan for Setbacks

Purpose of the Activity: The purpose of today's activity is to create a structured plan for dealing with setbacks when they occur. This plan will act as a roadmap to guide you through difficult times, ensuring that you have concrete steps to follow, which can help reduce anxiety and uncertainty. By having a coping plan in place, you can approach setbacks with a sense of preparedness and confidence, which is essential for overcoming obstacles more effectively. The coping plan also serves as a reminder of your resources and support options, making it easier to take constructive action rather than succumbing to negative emotions.

How to Engage in the Activity:

1.Identify Common Setbacks: Reflect on your journey so far and identify the types of setbacks you commonly encounter or anticipate facing. These might include slipping back into old habits, facing unusually stressful situations, or feeling overwhelmed by your emotions. Take the time to analyze when and why these setbacks typically occur. Understanding the triggers can help you anticipate and prepare for them more effectively. Consider not only the setbacks themselves but also any emotional or environmental factors that exacerbate these challenges. This broader perspective can be invaluable in developing more robust coping mechanisms.

2.Develop Specific Strategies: For each type of setback identified, develop specific strategies to cope. These strategies might include reaching out to your support network, engaging in relaxation techniques, or revisiting your therapy goals and achievements to gain perspective. Tailor these strategies to fit the specific challenges you face; for instance, if returning to old habits is a frequent issue, create a plan that focuses on reinforcing new, healthier patterns through rewards or accountability. If emotional overwhelm is common, you might prioritize strategies that help you manage your emotions, such as mindfulness or scheduled downtime.

3.Write Down Your Plan: Create a detailed document or journal entry outlining your coping strategies. This written plan should be easily accessible and include actionable steps you can take when faced with a setback. Include motivational reminders of why you started this journey and what you've accomplished so far. This documentation acts as a roadmap you can refer to in moments of doubt, providing clear instructions and reminders of the tools at your disposal. It also serves as a record of your proactive efforts to manage your mental health, reinforcing your commitment to personal growth.

4.Practice Scenarios: Role-play or mentally rehearse your responses to potential setbacks using your coping plan. This practice can help solidify your strategies and make them feel more natural to implement when needed. Visualization and mental rehearsal are powerful tools in habit formation; by imagining yourself successfully navigating setbacks, you build confidence in your ability to handle real-life situations. This preparation can reduce anxiety and improve your effectiveness in dealing with challenges.

5.Review and Revise: Regularly review your coping plan to ensure it remains relevant and effective. Adjust your strategies as you learn more about what works best for you in managing setbacks. As you evolve, your needs and circumstances will change, requiring adjustments to your approaches. This ongoing process of review and revision ensures that your coping strategies grow with you and continue to serve your best interests. Schedule periodic reviews, such as at the end of each month or after any major life event, to reflect on your progress and make necessary changes. This habit of continuous improvement will help you maintain resilience and adaptability in the face of challenges.

Conclusion of Day 18

Today, by developing a coping plan for setbacks, you have equipped yourself with an essential tool for maintaining your mental health progress. This plan not only prepares you to deal with difficulties but also reinforces your commitment to your therapeutic goals. Remember, setbacks are not indicators of failure but are part of the normal ebb and flow of life. With a solid plan in place, you can face these challenges head-on and continue moving forward with confidence and resilience. Keep refining your strategies as you grow and learn, allowing each experience to strengthen rather than hinder your progress. This ongoing process ensures that you are always prepared and responsive, rather than reactive, making you better equipped to handle future challenges.

N O T E S

Day 19: Mindfulness Advanced Techniques

Objective

Day 19 is dedicated to advancing your mindfulness practice, focusing specifically on integrating mindfulness into everyday activities such as walking. The objective today is to deepen your mindfulness skills by learning to maintain awareness and presence in more dynamic settings, beyond seated or static meditation. This practice, known as mindfulness walking, helps embed mindfulness more thoroughly into your daily life, enhancing your ability to stay centered and calm in various situations. By learning to extend mindfulness to walking, a common daily activity, you transform a routine action into a profound exercise in awareness, which can significantly improve your mental clarity and reduce stress levels.

Overview

Mindfulness walking is a form of meditation in motion that involves focusing on the experience of walking, noticing the sensations in your body, and observing your environment without judgment. This technique can be particularly beneficial for those who find traditional meditation challenging or prefer more active forms of mindfulness. It allows for the cultivation of a calm, meditative state while engaging in a physical activity, merging the benefits of exercise with mindfulness. This form of active meditation emphasizes the connection between physical movement and mental health, offering a versatile method of stress relief that can be practiced almost anywhere.

Activity: Mindfulness Walking

Purpose of the Activity: The purpose of today's activity is to practice mindfulness in a more active setting, helping to strengthen your ability to apply mindfulness techniques in all areas of life. Mindfulness walking is an excellent way to connect the mind and body, encouraging a state of enhanced awareness and presence. This practice not only promotes relaxation and stress reduction but also improves your physical well-being by incorporating gentle exercise. Engaging in mindfulness walking regularly can lead to greater emotional resilience, as you learn to navigate and remain calm through the everyday flux of mental and environmental stimuli.

How to Engage in the Activity:

1.**Choose Your Environment:** Select a location for your mindfulness walk. This could be a quiet park, a garden, or even a less trafficked path in your neighborhood. Ideally, choose a place that is relatively peaceful and where you can walk without too many interruptions. The setting plays a crucial role in the quality of your practice, as a calm and beautiful environment can significantly enhance your focus and enjoyment.

2.**Start with Intention:** Begin your walk with the clear intention of being mindful. Take a few moments to stand still, breathe deeply, and commit to maintaining focus on the present moment throughout your walk. This initial moment of intention sets a purposeful tone for your activity, grounding you in your mindfulness goals.

3.**Engage All Your Senses:** As you start walking, pay close attention to the physical sensations of walking – the feel of your feet touching the ground, the rhythm of your stride, and the movement of your arms. Expand your awareness to include the sounds around you, the temperature of the air, and anything you can smell. If your mind wanders, gently bring your attention back to these sensations. This sensory engagement is crucial in cultivating a deep sense of presence, pulling you away from the habitual chatter of the mind.

4.**Observe Without Judgement:** Try to observe your surroundings without forming judgments. If you notice your mind labeling or evaluating what you see, gently redirect your focus back to the simple act of walking and the sensations associated with it. This practice of non-judgment is fundamental in mindfulness and helps cultivate a more open and accepting attitude towards life.

5.Conclude with Reflection: End your walk with a few minutes standing or sitting quietly, reflecting on the experience. Consider how your body feels compared to before the walk and any changes in your mental state. This reflection helps to consolidate the benefits of your mindfulness practice and provides insights into the effects of your efforts.

Conclusion of Day 19

Mindfulness walking on Day 19 has expanded your toolkit for practicing mindfulness, adding a dynamic and practical technique that can be integrated into your daily routine. This activity not only enhances your physical health but also promotes a deeper connection between your mind and body, fostering a state of awareness that can greatly benefit your overall well-being. As you continue to practice mindfulness walking, you may find it becomes a valuable part of your strategy for managing stress and staying grounded in the present moment, no matter where you are or what you are doing. Over time, this practice can lead to significant improvements in your ability to focus, relax, and enjoy a richer, more connected experience of daily life.

NOTES

Day 20: Self-Care Strategies

Objective

Day 20 is dedicated to emphasizing the importance of self-care in maintaining and enhancing mental health. The goal for today is to identify and plan personal self-care activities that cater to both physical and emotional well-being. Effective self-care strategies can significantly influence overall life satisfaction, resilience against stress, and the ability to manage anxiety and depression. By developing a comprehensive personal self-care plan, you can ensure that you regularly engage in activities that rejuvenate and sustain you, providing a stable foundation for mental health. This proactive approach not only helps in coping with existing stressors but also in preventing the onset of stress-related issues, fostering a healthier lifestyle overall.

Overview

Self-care encompasses a variety of activities that nurture your health and well-being, ranging from physical care like sleep and exercise, to emotional and psychological care such as relaxation techniques and hobbies. Understanding and implementing effective self-care strategies is crucial because it helps prevent burnout, reduces the impact of stress, and supports recovery processes. Furthermore, self-care promotes a positive relationship with oneself, enhancing self-esteem and fostering a proactive attitude towards health. It teaches the importance of setting boundaries, prioritizing personal needs, and the value of treating oneself with kindness and respect.

Activity: Developing a Personal Self-Care Plan

Purpose of the Activity: The purpose of today's activity is to design a personalized self-care plan that addresses your specific needs and preferences. This plan should be holistic, covering various aspects of self-care including physical, emotional, social, and intellectual dimensions. By having a structured plan, you are more likely to implement regular self-care practices, which can improve your overall quality of life and your ability to handle the demands of daily life. Crafting this plan encourages a thorough self-assessment, prompting you to reflect deeply on what truly nourishes you and what aspects of your life require more attention and nurturing.

How to Engage in the Activity:

1.Assessment of Needs: Start by assessing your current self-care practices and identifying areas that need more attention. Consider aspects of your life where you feel lacking or areas that cause you stress and think about what kinds of activities could help mitigate these issues. This evaluation helps in pinpointing specific stressors and tailoring your self-care practices to address them effectively.

2.Listing Self-Care Activities: Create a list of activities that you enjoy or find relaxing and rejuvenating. These might include things like reading, yoga, spending time in nature, having dinner with friends, or taking time each day to meditate.

Be sure to consider activities that engage different aspects of your well-being. Including a variety of activities ensures a balanced approach, catering to your comprehensive health needs.

3.Scheduling: Plan how and when you can incorporate these activities into your daily or weekly routine. It's important to set realistic goals that fit into your schedule without causing additional stress. For example, if finding an hour for yoga is too challenging, consider shorter, more frequent activities like taking a 10-minute walk or doing a 5-minute stretching session. Setting a schedule helps create a routine, making it more likely that you'll stick to your self-care plan.

4.Flexibility and Adaptability: While it's crucial to have a plan, it's equally important to remain flexible and willing to adjust your self-care practices as your needs and circumstances change. Periodically review and adjust your plan to ensure it continues to meet your needs effectively. This adaptability is key to maintaining an effective self-care routine that genuinely supports your well-being.

5.Commitment and Reflection: Commit to your self-care plan and regularly reflect on how these practices affect your mental and physical health. Take note of what works well and what doesn't, and feel free to modify your plan accordingly. Reflecting on the benefits of your self-care regimen can also reinforce your motivation to maintain it. Regular reflection allows for continuous improvement and ensures your self-care activities remain relevant and beneficial.

Conclusion of Day 20

Developing a personal self-care plan today is a significant step toward taking control of your well-being. By identifying and scheduling regular activities that promote health and relaxation, you are creating a foundation for lasting mental health and resilience. Self-care is an ongoing process, and your plan will likely evolve as you discover what most effectively helps you to relax, recharge, and stay balanced. Remember, the purpose of self-care is to maintain a harmonious balance that supports both your physical and mental health, enabling you to thrive in all areas of life. As you integrate these practices into your daily routine, you'll likely find an improvement in your overall mood, energy levels, and productivity.

N O T E S

Day 21: Reflection and Review

The third week culminates with a day dedicated to reflection and review, a key component to consolidating the skills and strategies developed over the past days. This reflective practice allows for a deeper understanding of how the newly integrated techniques, such as Behavioral Activation, advanced mindfulness, and structured self-care plans, are impacting your mental health and everyday life. By taking the time to reflect, you can evaluate the effectiveness of these strategies, identify areas for further improvement, and reinforce your commitment to ongoing personal growth.

Reflecting on your experiences provides an opportunity to acknowledge your progress and recalibrate your approach as needed. It's a moment to celebrate successes, learn from challenges, and plan future steps with greater insight and precision.

Reflect on the Week's Progress and Journal Insights:

Summarize Each Day's Focus: Begin by revisiting the focus of each day this week. Recall the introduction of Behavioral Activation on Day 15, the practice of SMART goal setting on Day 16, the deepening of your mindfulness techniques on Day 17, the strategic coping for setbacks on Day 18, and your creation of a personal self-care plan on Day 20.

Evaluate Your Experiences: Reflect on how these activities influenced your mood, anxiety levels, and overall well-being. Which techniques were most beneficial? How did the integration of these strategies impact your daily interactions and personal productivity?

Identify Patterns and Insights: Look for patterns in how you responded to the different techniques introduced. Which practices did you find most challenging, and which seemed to resonate deeply with your needs? Understanding these patterns can help tailor your ongoing practice to be more effective.

Plan for Future Application: Based on your reflections, determine areas that require more focus or adjustment. Consider how you can further incorporate these strategies into your routine to continue supporting your mental health. For instance, if Behavioral Activation significantly improved your mood, think about how you can expand these activities into other areas of your life.

Set Goals for the Upcoming Week: Outline specific goals for the next week, building on the progress made. These goals should reflect both your long-term aspirations and the immediate steps needed to continue your growth and development in managing anxiety and enhancing overall well-being.

Conclusion of Day 21

Reflecting on the week's progress and journaling insights have helped solidify the benefits of the techniques practiced and provided clarity on your path forward. This process is invaluable as it not only confirms the value of the methods used but also enhances your ability to apply these techniques autonomously in the future. Continue to engage with these reflective practices regularly to maintain awareness of your mental health status and to adaptively manage your strategies for optimal well-being. As you move into future weeks, use today's reflections to keep your approach dynamic and responsive to your evolving needs, ensuring sustained progress and resilience.

IV

Week 4: Consolidation and Future Planning

"The best way to predict your future is to create it." - Peter Drucker

Day 22: Combining Techniques

Objective

Day 22 marks the beginning of the fourth week, focusing on consolidating the skills and techniques learned in the previous weeks. The objective today is to effectively combine various CBT techniques into a cohesive daily routine. By integrating these strategies seamlessly into your day-to-day activities, you can maximize their effectiveness and ensure that they become a sustainable part of your lifestyle. This consolidation helps to reinforce the habits that contribute to ongoing mental health improvements and resilience against stress and anxiety.

Overview

Combining CBT techniques involves synchronizing methods like mindfulness, behavioral activation, SMART goals, and self-care into a routine that supports continuous mental health management. This integrated approach allows for the reinforcement of each technique through its interaction with others, enhancing overall efficacy. By creating a routine that incorporates multiple strategies, you ensure that you are addressing various aspects of your mental health comprehensively, from stress management and positive thinking to goal setting and proactive self-care.

Activity: Integrating Learned CBT Techniques into a Daily Routine

Purpose of the Activity: The purpose of today's activity is to develop a personalized daily routine that incorporates the CBT techniques you've learned and practiced. This integration aims to make these techniques more accessible and actionable in everyday contexts, ensuring that you have a robust set of tools at your disposal to manage different situations effectively. Structuring your day around these practices can also help establish consistency, which is crucial for the techniques to become habitual and for their benefits to be fully realized.

How to Engage in the Activity:

1.Review Learned Techniques: Take some time to reflect on the various CBT techniques you've learned recently. From mindfulness exercises to gratitude journaling, make a comprehensive list of all the strategies you've been introduced to. Consider how each technique has resonated with you and which ones you've found particularly helpful in managing stress and improving your mental well-being.

2.Create a Daily Schedule: Once you've compiled your list of CBT techniques, it's time to integrate them into your daily routine. Start by mapping out a typical day and identifying where you can naturally incorporate these practices. For instance, you may discover that practicing mindfulness meditation in the morning helps set a positive tone for the day, while dedicating time in the evening to gratitude journaling allows you to reflect on moments of appreciation. Consider how you can schedule activities like exercise or engaging in hobbies at specific times to optimize their impact on your mood and energy levels.

3.Plan for Flexibility: While having a structured routine is important, it's equally crucial to build flexibility into your schedule. Life often throws unexpected curveballs, and rigid routines can sometimes exacerbate stress rather than alleviate it. Incorporate alternative options into your schedule for days when your usual activities aren't feasible. This could involve shorter mindfulness practices during busy periods or adjusting the timing of certain activities to accommodate unexpected events without derailing your entire day.

4.Implement the Routine: Once you've established your schedule, begin implementing it into your daily life. Pay close attention to how each integration point reinforces the effectiveness of the other techniques. Notice how practicing mindfulness meditation in the morning enhances your ability to engage in gratitude journaling later in the day, for example. As you follow your routine, be mindful of any adjustments you may need to make to optimize its effectiveness based on your individual preferences and experiences.

5.Regularly Review and Adjust: Set aside time at regular intervals, such as once a month, to review your routine and assess its effectiveness. Take stock of what's working well and what could be improved, and be open to making adjustments as needed. This ongoing process of reflection and refinement is essential for ensuring that your CBT practices remain relevant and impactful in addressing your mental health needs. By regularly reviewing and adjusting your routine, you can continue to evolve and optimize your approach to self-care and well-being.

Conclusion of Day 22

By the end of Day 22, you will have created a comprehensive daily routine that integrates the various CBT techniques you've learned. This structured approach not only aids in the consolidation of these methods into your everyday life but also ensures that they continue to support your mental health goals in the long term. As you move forward, this routine will help you maintain a balanced and proactive approach to managing your mental health, equipping you with the tools needed to handle challenges effectively and maintain your well-being.

NOTES

131

Day 23: Maintaining Gains

Objective

Day 23 is focused on maintaining the gains achieved through the CBT techniques learned and practiced over the past few weeks. The goal for today is to ensure that these improvements are sustained over the long term, particularly in the face of future challenges and stressors. This involves proactive planning and preparation for potential situations that could trigger stress or relapse, enhancing your resilience and ability to stay on course with your mental health goals. This stage is critical as it shifts the focus from initial recovery to long-term maintenance, ensuring that the skills learned are not just temporary fixes but part of a permanent lifestyle change.

Overview

Maintaining gains in any therapeutic process requires an understanding of the factors that contribute to continued success as well as those that pose risks. It's essential to recognize that while progress can be made, the journey often includes navigating setbacks and maintaining vigilance against old patterns of behavior. Today's focus is on reinforcing the coping strategies that have been effective for you and identifying new strategies to deal with future challenges, ensuring that your achievements are not only protected but also built upon. This proactive approach helps you to not feel overwhelmed by future stressors and instead view them as manageable challenges that can be tackled with the right tools.

Activity: Identifying and Planning for Potential Future Stressors

Purpose of the Activity: The purpose of today's activity is to identify potential future stressors and plan effective strategies for managing them. This forward-thinking approach is crucial for preventing relapse and for building confidence in your ability to handle challenges without compromising your mental health progress. By anticipating possible difficulties and preparing for them, you can approach future challenges with a sense of readiness and empowerment. The activity encourages a mindset of resilience, adapting the skills you've learned to specific future contexts and reinforcing your ability to navigate life's uncertainties.

How to Engage in the Activity:

1.Identify Potential Stressors: Reflect on past experiences and current fears to list potential future stressors. These might include specific events like job changes or personal milestones, or more general concerns like managing work-life balance or dealing with family dynamics. When listing these stressors, consider not only the obvious triggers but also subtler sources of stress that may accumulate over time. Understanding both acute and chronic sources of stress will enable you to prepare more comprehensively. It's important to consider not just the external events but also internal pressures and expectations that could contribute to stress.

2.Analyze Previous Responses: Look at how you have previously handled similar stressors and identify what strategies were effective and what aspects could have been improved. This reflection helps you understand your strengths and areas where new strategies might be needed. Evaluate both your emotional and practical responses to these situations. Were there patterns in your reactions that might point to habitual responses? Recognizing these can be instrumental in breaking cycles of ineffective behavior and replacing them with more constructive actions.

3.Develop Coping Strategies: For each identified stressor, develop specific coping strategies based on the CBT techniques you've learned. This might include relaxation techniques for immediate stress relief, cognitive restructuring to address negative thoughts, or behavioral activation to ensure continued engagement in enjoyable activities. Tailor these strategies to the nuances of each stressor, considering the unique challenges it presents. For example, stressors that trigger anxiety might be best managed with techniques that calm the mind and body, while those that lead to procrastination might be more effectively addressed with strategies that enhance motivation and action.

4.Create an Action Plan: Develop a detailed action plan for each stressor that includes clear steps to take when faced with the stressor, resources you might need, and who in your support network you can rely on. This plan should be practical and easily accessible in times of stress. The more detailed your plan, the less thinking you'll have to do in a stressful moment, which can help reduce anxiety and increase effectiveness. Include contingency options in case your initial plan needs adjustment. This level of preparation can provide a significant psychological comfort.

5.Practice Scenarios: Where possible, role-play or mentally rehearse your response to potential stressors using your action plans. This practice can help reduce anxiety about unknowns and reinforce your confidence in handling challenging situations. If possible, involve a friend or family member in these role-plays to simulate interactions more realistically. The act of visualizing and practicing your response can make a significant difference in your ability to manage stress effectively when it arises.

6.Regular Review and Update: Commit to regularly reviewing and updating your plans for potential stressors. As circumstances change and as you grow, your strategies and needs may evolve. Keeping your plans current ensures they remain relevant and effective. Schedule these reviews at regular intervals—perhaps every few months or after any major life event. This not only helps in adapting to changes but also in reinforcing your commitment to proactive stress management.

Conclusion of Day 23

On Day 23, by identifying potential future stressors and planning how to manage them, you've taken a significant step towards ensuring the sustainability of your mental health gains. This proactive approach not only prepares you for future challenges but also reinforces your resilience, giving you the tools and confidence needed to maintain progress. By continually refining and practicing these plans, you enhance your ability to adapt to changes and effectively manage stress, which is vital for sustained mental health and well-being. This ongoing vigilance and preparation are key to not only surviving but thriving in the face of life's challenges.

N O T E S

137

Day 24: Enhancing Resilience

Objective

Day 24 focuses on enhancing resilience, a critical aspect of maintaining long-term mental health and effectively managing stress and adversity. The objective today is to strengthen your ability to bounce back from challenges and adapt to change with less difficulty. By building resilience, you equip yourself to handle both everyday stresses and significant life events with greater ease and confidence, ensuring that setbacks are managed constructively and do not lead to prolonged distress. Enhancing resilience is integral because it involves not only recovery from difficulties but also fortifying oneself against future challenges, promoting a more enduring and robust approach to personal well-being.

Overview

Resilience involves a combination of personal qualities and learned skills that enable individuals to thrive in the face of adversity. It includes maintaining a positive outlook, managing emotions effectively, and seeing failures as opportunities for growth. Enhancing resilience is crucial because it extends beyond coping with the present; it prepares you for future challenges and helps prevent the development of mental health difficulties. This day is dedicated to developing strategies that foster resilience, emphasizing the importance of proactive mental health management and personal growth. By committing to these practices, you can create a life that not only withstands storms but also grows more robust through them.

Activity: Techniques for Building Long-Term Resilience

Purpose of the Activity: The purpose of today's activity is to explore and practice techniques that can help build and enhance your long-term resilience. These techniques are designed to fortify your psychological and emotional defenses, equipping you to navigate life's ups and downs more effectively. By strengthening your resilience, you can improve your overall well-being and maintain progress in your mental health journey. Engaging in resilience-building activities helps integrate these practices into your daily life, making them second nature and more effective when confronted with stress or adversity.

How to Engage in the Activity:

1.Identify Sources of Strength: Start by identifying your current sources of strength in times of stress. These can include supportive relationships, past successes, personal skills, or positive attributes. Recognizing these resources can boost your confidence and remind you of your capabilities when faced with future challenges. Acknowledging these strengths also reinforces your self-esteem, which is vital for resilience.

2.Develop a Growth Mindset: Practice developing a growth mindset by reframing how you view challenges and failures. Instead of seeing them as insurmountable obstacles, view them as opportunities to learn and grow. Focus on what can be gained from every situation, and remind yourself that skills and abilities can be developed through effort and persistence. This mindset encourages persistence and optimism in the face of challenges, essential qualities for resilience.

3.Build Emotional Awareness: Enhance your ability to identify and manage your emotions by practicing mindfulness and emotional regulation techniques. Being able to stay calm and composed under stress is a key component of resilience. Greater emotional awareness allows for more effective communication and decision-making under pressure.

4.Strengthen Social Connections: Actively work to strengthen your social network by reaching out to friends, family, and colleagues. Strong, positive relationships are a cornerstone of resilience, providing emotional support and practical assistance in difficult times. These connections offer a buffer against psychological stress, ensuring you have a supportive community to lean on when needed.

5.Create a Resilience Plan: Develop a personal resilience plan that outlines how to use these techniques in challenging situations. Include specific steps to take when you feel overwhelmed, resources you can draw on, and ways to remind yourself of your resilience in the face of adversity. This structured approach ensures you have clear strategies to implement, enhancing your ability to cope effectively.

6.Regular Practice: Commit to regular practice of these techniques. Resilience builds over time through consistent effort and application. Set aside time each week to reflect on your resilience practices and their impact on your life. Regular practice not only deepens your resilience but also makes these strategies more readily available in times of need.

Conclusion of Day 24

By focusing on enhancing resilience, Day 24 helps solidify your ability to manage stress and recover from setbacks effectively. The techniques explored today are essential tools for building a robust psychological foundation that supports long-term mental health. As you continue to strengthen your resilience, you'll find yourself more capable of handling whatever life throws your way, not just surviving but thriving in the face of challenges. Continue to nurture and develop these skills, as they are vital for sustained well-being and personal growth. This ongoing commitment to building resilience will serve as your foundation for future success and happiness.

NOTES

Day 25: Review of Mindfulness Practice

Objective

Day 25 is devoted to a thorough review and enhancement of your mindfulness practice. The objective is to consolidate your mindfulness skills, reflect on how they have been integrated into your daily life, and explore ways to deepen these practices. By revisiting and refining your mindfulness techniques, you can ensure they continue to be effective tools for managing stress, enhancing awareness, and promoting emotional and psychological well-being.

Overview

Mindfulness is a foundational skill in cognitive behavioral therapy and mental health maintenance that helps anchor you in the present moment, reducing stress and improving overall emotional regulation. This practice supports a variety of benefits, including reduced reactivity to stress, improved concentration, and enhanced relational well-being. Today's review aims to strengthen these outcomes by encouraging a deeper engagement with mindfulness exercises and integrating them more fully into different aspects of your daily routine.

Activity: Deepening Mindfulness Practice

Purpose of the Activity: The purpose of today's activity is to deepen your understanding and application of mindfulness. This involves not just continuing existing practices but also exploring new mindfulness techniques that can enhance your ability to remain present and calm under various circumstances. Enhancing your mindfulness practice can lead to greater emotional resilience and a more profound sense of peace in your daily life.

How to Engage in the Activity:

1.**Evaluate Current Practice:** Begin by evaluating your current mindfulness routine. Reflect on what techniques have been most effective and which aspects might still be challenging. Consider how often you practice, what times of day you engage in mindfulness, and how these factors influence the effectiveness of your practice. Assess whether your current practice aligns with your mental health goals and if it helps in areas you specifically want to improve, such as reducing anxiety or enhancing concentration. Also, think about the environment in which you practice mindfulness—does it contribute to or detract from your focus and relaxation? Understanding these nuances can help refine your approach, making your practice more beneficial and tailored to your needs.

2.Introduce New Techniques: Based on your evaluation, introduce new mindfulness techniques that might enhance your practice. This could include trying different forms of meditation like loving-kindness meditation, mindfulness-based stress reduction programs, or guided imagery exercises that focus on deepening relaxation and awareness. Exploring new techniques can keep your practice fresh and engaging, and may address different aspects of mindfulness that are particularly relevant to your current life circumstances. For instance, if you find yourself struggling with negative thoughts towards yourself or others, loving-kindness meditation can foster more positive attitudes and feelings of compassion.

3.Set Specific Goals: Establish specific goals for your deepened practice. For example, if you decide to incorporate loving-kindness meditation, set a goal to practice it for a certain number of minutes each day or include it in your routine a certain number of times per week. Goals should be realistic and tailored to fit into your lifestyle seamlessly. Specify what you hope to achieve with each new technique, such as improved emotional regulation, better sleep, or increased feelings of empathy. By setting clear, measurable goals, you give your practice direction and purpose, which can enhance motivation and commitment. Additionally, consider setting intermediate milestones that can help you gauge your progress and make adjustments as necessary.

4.Create a Dedicated Space: If possible, create or refine a dedicated space for your mindfulness practice. This space should be inviting and free from distractions, which can help signal to your brain that it is time to focus inwardly and engage in the practice fully. Consider elements that enhance calmness and concentration, such as soft lighting, comfortable seating, or calming colors. Adding personal touches like plants, inspirational quotes, or calming images can also make the space feel more personal and soothing. This dedicated space doesn't need to be large; even a small corner of a room can be transformed into a peaceful retreat that supports your mindfulness journey.

5.Practice Regularly: Commit to practicing mindfulness at regular intervals and track your progress. Regular practice is essential for deepening your mindfulness and making it a sustainable part of your life. Consider using a journal to note your experiences, feelings, and any insights that arise during practice. This record can be invaluable for tracking how your mindfulness practice evolves and identifying patterns or changes in your emotional or mental state over time. It also serves as a reflective tool, helping you to see how far you've come and motivating you to continue. Setting a regular schedule and adhering to it as much as possible helps to establish mindfulness as a habit, integrating it more deeply into your daily life.

6.Seek Feedback: If possible, seek feedback on your practice from a mindfulness coach, therapist, or through a mindfulness group. Feedback can provide new perspectives and suggestions for enhancing your practice and overcoming any obstacles you encounter. Engaging with a community or a professional can also provide support and encouragement, which are often crucial when facing challenges in your practice. They can offer accountability, which may motivate you to stick with your practice during periods of low motivation or when you are not seeing immediate benefits. Additionally, sharing experiences and learning from the experiences of others can introduce new practices or modifications that might be more effective for you.

Conclusion of Day 25

Today's review and enhancement of your mindfulness practice are vital for ensuring that these techniques continue to serve as effective tools for managing stress and improving mental health. By deepening your mindfulness practice, you not only enhance your ability to stay present and calm but also foster a deeper connection with yourself, which is essential for long-term emotional and psychological well-being. As you move forward, keep exploring new areas of mindfulness and integrating these practices more fully into all areas of your life, enhancing their benefits and your overall quality of life.

NOTES

Day 26: Finalizing the Support Network

Objective

Day 26 is devoted to finalizing and solidifying your support network, an essential element in sustaining the improvements gained through your mental health journey. The goal for today is to ensure that your relationships and support systems are robust, reliable, and responsive to your needs. This involves actively engaging with and reinforcing the bonds you have with family, friends, therapists, or support groups who play a critical role in your ongoing wellness.

Overview

A strong support network is crucial for long-term mental health maintenance because it provides emotional support, practical help, and a sense of belonging. Strengthening these relationships means ensuring that you have access to encouragement and advice when facing challenges. Today's focus will be on evaluating these relationships, enhancing communication, and setting boundaries where necessary to ensure that interactions remain healthy and supportive.

Activity: Solidifying Relationships and Support Systems

Purpose of the Activity: The purpose of today's activity is to actively engage in strengthening your relationships with those in your support network. This means not only ensuring that the relationships are supportive and positive but also that they are well-maintained and equipped to handle the ups and downs of your mental health journey. Solidifying these relationships ensures that you have a dependable and effective support system in place.

How to Engage in the Activity:

1.Evaluate Your Current Relationships: Start by evaluating the current state of your relationships within your support network. Identify which relationships provide the most support and which might need more attention or reevaluation. Consider the quality of support offered and how well these relationships meet your emotional and practical needs. Assess if there are any gaps in the type of support you require versus what is currently available. This might involve identifying relationships that have been overlooked or underutilized that could potentially be strengthened to provide additional support. Understanding these dynamics allows you to make informed decisions about where to invest your energy to fortify your support system.

2.Enhance Communication: Openly communicate your appreciation to those who have been supportive. Let them know how much their support means to you and discuss how you can continue to support each other effectively. For relationships that need improvement, consider discussing your needs more clearly or setting up regular check-ins to foster better communication. Effective communication can transform relationships, making them more resilient and supportive. It's important to be transparent about your feelings and any changes in your life that might affect your relationships, ensuring that your support network understands your current circumstances and needs.

3.Plan Reciprocal Support: Relationships thrive on reciprocity. Plan how you can be supportive to your network members, not just when you need support but also proactively. This might involve offering help, sharing resources, or simply spending quality time together. Think about the unique needs of each person in your network and how you can meet them. By doing so, you strengthen the bond and ensure that the support you give is meaningful and appreciated. This reciprocal approach not only enriches your relationships but also builds a deeper sense of community and mutual care within your network.

4.Set Healthy Boundaries: Setting healthy boundaries is essential for maintaining good relationships. Define what you are comfortable with in terms of emotional and practical engagements, and communicate these boundaries clearly to your support network. Explain why these boundaries are important to you and how they contribute to your well-being. It's crucial that these boundaries are respected by your network, as they protect your mental health and ensure that interactions remain supportive and not overwhelming or counterproductive.

5.Regular Engagement: Commit to regular engagement with your support network. Schedule regular meetings, calls, or activities that keep you connected. Staying engaged helps ensure that your relationships remain strong and supportive over the long term. Consistent contact not only keeps relationships vibrant but also makes it easier to reach out when support is needed, as regular communication builds trust and familiarity. Consider setting up a recurring schedule that works for everyone involved, whether it's weekly coffee meet-ups, monthly dinner gatherings, or simply checking in via text or calls at set times.

Conclusion of Day 26

Finalizing your support network on Day 26 is a vital step in ensuring that you have a reliable foundation of support for the future. By solidifying these relationships, you guarantee that you have a network of individuals who understand your needs and are prepared to assist you through any challenges. Regularly maintaining and nurturing these relationships will strengthen your overall resilience and ability to manage your mental health effectively. Keep these connections active, and ensure they are mutually supportive, to maintain a healthy and robust support network.

153

NOTES

Day 27: Preparing for the Future

Objective

Day 27 is dedicated to preparing for the future, with a specific focus on creating a long-term plan for maintaining anxiety reduction. This objective is crucial as it extends the benefits of the Cognitive Behavioral Therapy (CBT) techniques and mindfulness practices learned over the past weeks into enduring habits that support sustained mental health. The goal is to establish a proactive approach that not only manages anxiety but also prevents its escalation, ensuring that you can continue to thrive in various life circumstances.

Overview

Preparing for the future in the context of mental health involves anticipating potential stressors and having a clear, structured plan to manage them without letting them undermine your well-being. This approach requires a comprehensive understanding of the triggers that exacerbate your anxiety, the strategies that have effectively mitigated it, and how these strategies can be adapted and incorporated into your daily life over the long term.

Activity: Creating a Long-term Plan for Maintaining Anxiety Reduction

Purpose of the Activity: The purpose of today's activity is to create a structured, detailed plan that outlines how you will continue to manage and reduce anxiety in the long term. This plan should utilize the insights and skills you have developed throughout your CBT sessions and ensure that they remain a central part of your mental health regimen. By developing a clear plan, you reinforce your commitment to ongoing self-care and mental health maintenance, which is key to long-term well-being.

How to Engage in the Activity:

1.Review Effective Strategies: Begin by reviewing the strategies and techniques that have been most effective in reducing your anxiety during the therapy. This could include mindfulness practices, behavioral activation, cognitive restructuring, or specific coping mechanisms for handling stress. Reflect on how each technique has impacted your day-to-day life and pinpoint those that provided the most significant relief or improvement in your mood and anxiety levels. Consider the context in which these strategies were most effective and whether any adjustments are needed to enhance their efficacy based on your current life situation.

2.Identify Triggers: Clearly identify potential triggers that could increase your anxiety in the future. Understanding these triggers allows you to tailor your plan to address them specifically, enhancing the effectiveness of your interventions. This step is crucial for preventing relapse and for maintaining control over your mental health. Delve into both common and personal triggers, categorizing them by their source, such as work-related, social interactions, health concerns, or financial issues, to ensure a comprehensive approach to your anxiety management.

3.Develop Routine Practices: Incorporate routine practices into your plan that support anxiety management. This might involve daily mindfulness exercises, regular physical activity, or scheduled times each week dedicated to relaxation and self-reflection. Consistency in these practices is key to their effectiveness, so consider integrating them into your daily schedule at times when you are most likely to follow through. For instance, you might find it beneficial to start your day with meditation to set a calm tone, or to include physical activity in the afternoon to manage energy and stress levels effectively.

4.Plan for Trigger Responses: For each identified trigger, develop a specific response plan that includes the steps you will take to mitigate anxiety when confronted with these situations. This could involve breathing exercises, reaching out to your support network, or engaging in an activity that distracts and calms you. Be as specific as possible in outlining these steps, ensuring that your plan is actionable and practical. For example, if public speaking is a trigger, your plan could include rehearsing extensively, using calming techniques right before speaking, and setting up a reward for yourself afterward to create positive associations.

5.Establish a Review Schedule: Set up a regular schedule to review and adjust your plan as needed. This ensures that your anxiety management strategies remain effective and responsive to your changing needs. Regular reviews can be monthly or quarterly and should involve assessing the success of your strategies and making adjustments based on what is or isn't working. This might mean adding new techniques, phasing out less effective ones, or adjusting the frequency and duration of practices based on your evolving circumstances.

6.Document Your Plan: Write down your plan in a clear, accessible format. Having a physical document or a digital file that outlines your strategies makes it easier to follow and ensures you have a ready reference when needed. This documentation should be easy to update as you refine and adapt your strategies over time. Additionally, consider creating reminders in your digital calendar or setting alerts on your phone to help keep you accountable to your plan and ensure that you don't overlook any critical components of your anxiety management routine.

Conclusion of Day 27

By creating a long-term plan for maintaining anxiety reduction, you are taking a significant step towards ensuring sustained mental health. This plan acts as a roadmap for navigating future challenges and reinforces the skills and habits you've developed during your therapy sessions. As you move forward, keep in mind that the ultimate goal is not just to manage anxiety but to enhance your overall quality of life, enabling you to engage more fully in all aspects of your personal and professional life.

NOTES

Days 28-30: Reflection, Review, and Celebration

Objective

The final days of the program are dedicated to reflection, review, and celebration of the journey you have undertaken. These days serve to consolidate your learning, assess the progress made, and reinforce the commitment to continue using the strategies and techniques that have proven effective. The aim is to create a sustainable practice that will support your mental health over the long term. This closing phase is critical as it transitions you from a structured program to independent management of your ongoing mental health, equipping you with the confidence and tools necessary to continue your progress independently.

Overview

Reflecting on the entire journey allows you to see the comprehensive changes that have occurred, appreciate the effort you have invested, and understand the significance of continuing these practices. Reviewing your progress helps identify the most beneficial aspects of the therapy and ensures that these can be integrated into your daily life moving forward. Celebrating your achievements is crucial as it recognizes the hard work and progress made, boosting your motivation to maintain these gains. It also serves as an uplifting reminder of your capabilities and the effective strategies you now have at your disposal to manage future challenges.

Activities: Reflection, Review, and Celebration

Purpose of the Activities: These activities are designed to end the program on a note of success and optimism. By taking the time to reflect and review, you solidify the knowledge and skills acquired. Celebrating your achievements emphasizes the positive changes and reinforces your confidence in managing your mental health. This structured reflection process not only deepens your understanding of what works best for you but also enhances your ability to apply these insights in real-life situations, ensuring that you remain proactive about your mental health.

How to Engage in the Activities:

1.Reflect on the Entire Journey:

Assess Changes: Consider how you felt at the beginning of the program versus now. Reflect on changes in your attitude, understanding, and management of anxiety. Note the specific moments or phases during the program when you felt a significant shift in your perspective or a decrease in your anxiety levels. This reflection allows you to see the tangible results of your efforts and can serve as a powerful motivator to continue applying the techniques you've learned.

Identify Key Lessons: Pinpoint the key lessons that had the most profound impact on your well-being. Recognize the strategies that helped you the most and contemplate how they can be incorporated into your routine. Reflecting in this manner helps you to internalize the progress you've made, making it easier to maintain these changes long-term. This process of identification helps in anchoring these lessons in your daily life, ensuring that they remain at the forefront of your mind as you move forward.

2.Review Progress and Plan for Continuity:

Evaluate Progress: Review the goals you set at the beginning and evaluate how well you have achieved them. Look at each technique you learned and assess its effectiveness in your daily life. This evaluation should be as detailed as possible, noting not only successes but also areas where expectations were not met, providing a balanced view of your progress.

Plan for Future Application: Decide how you will continue to apply these techniques. Consider setting new goals or adjusting your current strategies to fit your lifestyle better as it evolves. Planning for continuity is crucial as it sets the stage for ongoing self-improvement and ensures that the benefits of the therapy are not lost over time. This planning should also include strategies for adapting to potential life changes that could impact your routine, such as changes in employment, family dynamics, or physical health.

3.Celebrate Achievements:

Recognize Efforts: Acknowledge the hard work you have put into your mental health journey. This might involve a small personal celebration or sharing your achievements with friends, family, or your support network. Recognizing your effort is crucial in building self-esteem and furthering your commitment to your mental health.

Incentivize Future Commitment: Consider rewards that can keep you motivated to maintain these practices. This could be anything from new wellness tools (like a meditation app subscription) to activities that you enjoy (such as a retreat or a hobby-related class). Celebrating in this way not only marks your achievements but also reinforces the positive behaviors and practices you've developed, encouraging their continuation. Additionally, setting up a system of regular rewards for continued practice can help keep these habits a priority in your life, ensuring ongoing engagement and motivation.

Conclusion of Days 28-30

These final days are a crucial part of your therapy program, offering a chance to consolidate everything you have learned and prepare for continuing on your own. The reflections and reviews provide a clear picture of how far you have come and what still needs attention. Celebrating your achievements not only marks the completion of the program but also bolsters your self-esteem and dedication to ongoing self-care. As you move forward, keep the momentum going by regularly revisiting the techniques and strategies that have become integral to your daily routine. This ongoing practice will ensure that the benefits of your hard work are maintained and that your mental health continues to thrive, equipped with a robust set of tools for self-management and improvement.

* * *

Keeping the Game Alive

Now you have everything you need to conquer anxiety and unlock a life of peace and fulfillment, it's time to pass on your newfound knowledge and show other readers where they can find the same help.

Simply by leaving your honest opinion of this book on Amazon, you'll show other readers struggling with anxiety where they can find the information they're looking for, and pass their journey toward tranquility forward.

Thank you for your help. The journey to managing anxiety is kept alive when we pass on our knowledge – and you're helping us to do just that.

>> Click here to leave your review on Amazon or scan the QR Code below.

V

Conclusion

Summarizing Key Points

The journey through this program has been rich with growth, learning, and self-discovery, each step designed to equip you with the tools necessary for managing your mental health effectively. As we conclude, it's important to summarize the key points that have been central to this transformative process:

1.**Understanding and Applying CBT Techniques**: You've learned how cognitive-behavioral therapy (CBT) can be applied to manage anxiety and other emotional challenges. Techniques such as cognitive restructuring, behavioral activation, and mindfulness have been explored in depth, providing you with a robust toolkit for dealing with negative thought patterns and behaviors.

2.**Developing Mindfulness and Resilience**: Enhancing your mindfulness practices has allowed you to experience the present moment more fully, reducing stress and increasing overall mental clarity. Additionally, focusing on building resilience has prepared you to handle future challenges more effectively, ensuring that you can maintain your mental health gains over time.

3.Creating and Sustaining a Support Network: We emphasized the importance of solidifying a support network, which is crucial for long-term success. By strengthening relationships and ensuring you have reliable sources of support, you are better prepared to manage life's ups and downs.

4.Planning for the Future: The program has guided you in creating a detailed, long-term plan for maintaining your mental health. This plan includes strategies for continuing the practices you've learned, ensuring that you can sustain the progress made and continue to develop your mental health management skills.

5.Celebration of Achievements: Recognizing and celebrating your progress has been a key element, encouraging ongoing commitment to your mental health journey. Celebrations serve as milestones that acknowledge your hard work and reinforce the positive changes you've implemented.

As you move forward, remember that mental health management is an ongoing process. The techniques and strategies you've learned should be viewed as part of a long-term commitment to your well-being. Regularly revisiting these practices, adapting them as your life changes, and continuing to set and achieve new goals will help ensure that you remain on a path toward sustained mental health and happiness.

In conclusion, the journey you've embarked on is not just about overcoming immediate challenges but also about building a foundation for lasting mental health. The skills, knowledge, and insights gained are tools that will continue to serve you well into the future. Keep striving, keep learning, and remember that every step you take is a step toward a healthier, more fulfilled life.

Encouragement for Ongoing Practice

As you progress beyond the structured framework of this program, the importance of ongoing practice cannot be overstated. The journey to improved mental health is continuous, and the practices you've learned are not merely solutions to overcome temporary challenges but are skills to cultivate for a lifetime. Here are some encouraging thoughts and tips to help you maintain the momentum and keep your mental health practices vibrant and effective:

1. **View Practice as a Lifestyle**: Integrating the techniques into your daily life as a permanent lifestyle change rather than a temporary fix will make it easier to maintain them. Mindfulness, cognitive restructuring, and self-care should become as routine as eating well or exercising. Just as you nurture your body, so too must you continually nurture your mind.

2. **Set Gradual Goals**: Keep setting new, achievable goals for yourself. These can be small, incremental steps that build on the progress you've already made. Each small success will boost your confidence and reinforce the value of your ongoing efforts. Remember, improvement in mental health is often subtle, and continuous practice ensures

these small gains accumulate into significant changes.

3. **Stay Connected with Your Support Network**: Regularly engage with your support network not just during times of need but also to share successes and insights. This ongoing interaction can provide both motivation and joy, enhancing the benefits of your social connections.

4. **Keep Learning and Adapting**: The field of mental health is always evolving, with new research and techniques continually emerging. Stay curious and open to learning new strategies or deepening your understanding of current ones. This can also help renew your interest and commitment to practice.

5. **Reflect Regularly**: Make it a habit to periodically reflect on your mental health journey. Recognize how far you've come and acknowledge the effort it has taken to get here. Reflection can also help you identify areas that may need more attention or adjustment.

6. **Celebrate Continuously**: Just as we emphasized the importance of celebrating your achievements at the end of the program, it's crucial to continue celebrating your ongoing efforts and successes. Celebrating isn't just about acknowledging big milestones; it's also about appreciating the everyday victories that contribute to your overall well-being.

7. **Be Patient and Kind to Yourself**: There will be days when it feels difficult to practice, or when progress seems slow. It's important during these times to be patient and kind to yourself. Mental health improvement is not linear and expecting constant progress is unrealistic. Accept that there will be ups and downs, and treat yourself with compassion through both.

By keeping these points in mind and continuing to engage with the practices you've learned, you are setting yourself up for sustained success. Your commitment to ongoing practice is not just an investment in your mental health but an investment in your overall quality of life. Remember, every step forward, no matter how small, is a step towards a more resilient and fulfilled you.

Additional Resources and Further Reading

To support your ongoing journey in managing and enhancing your mental health, it's beneficial to have access to a variety of resources. These can offer deeper insights, provide different perspectives, and introduce new techniques to enrich your understanding and practices. Here are some suggested resources and further reading to help you continue learning and growing:

Books on Cognitive Behavioral Therapy (CBT) and Mindfulness:

- *Feeling Good: The New Mood Therapy* by David D. Burns - Offers practical advice and exercises based on CBT principles.
- *Wherever You Go, There You Are* by Jon Kabat-Zinn - A guide to mindfulness meditation and its applications in everyday life.
- *The Happiness Trap* by Russ Harris - Introduces Acceptance and Commitment Therapy (ACT), a mindfulness-based approach to managing negative thoughts and feelings.

Online Courses:

- Coursera and Udemy offer various courses on mental health topics, including mindfulness, psychological well-being, and stress management. These platforms often feature courses taught by university professors or experienced practitioners.
- Apps like Headspace and Calm provide guided meditation sessions that can enhance daily mindfulness practice.

Podcasts and Videos:

- *The Mental Illness Happy Hour* - A podcast that explores mental illness, trauma, addiction, and negative thinking.
- TED Talks on mental health topics - These can be inspiring and offer insights into personal stories and cutting-edge research in the field.

Professional Journals and Articles:

- Keep up-to-date with the latest research by reading professional journals such as *The Journal of Cognitive Psychotherapy* or *The American Journal of Psychiatry*. Many journals offer free articles or summaries that can be accessed online.

Support Groups and Workshops:

- Consider joining support groups, either in-person or online. Organizations like the Anxiety and Depression Association of America (ADAA) offer resources and tools to find local groups or online meetings.
- Workshops or group therapy sessions can also be a great way to learn new strategies and connect with others who

are working through similar issues.

Therapeutic Tools and Workbooks:

- *The Anxiety and Worry Workbook: The Cognitive Behavioral Solution* by David A. Clark and Aaron T. Beck - Provides practical exercises and insights for managing anxiety.
- *Mind Over Mood: Change How You Feel by Changing the Way You Think* by Dennis Greenberger and Christine Padesky - A workbook offering step-by-step guidance in cognitive therapy techniques.

By integrating these resources into your regular learning and practice routines, you can continue to expand your knowledge base and toolkit for mental health management. These resources not only provide education but also offer comfort and inspiration, reminding you that you are not alone in your journey. Regular engagement with a broad range of materials can enrich your understanding and support sustained growth and wellness.

www.ingramcontent.com/pod-product-compliance
Lightning Source LLC
Chambersburg PA
CBHW051603250726

48653CB00004BA/1308